YOUR TRUE KINGDOM

Identity

THE MAJESTY WITHIN

ROBERT JONES

Copyright Robert Jones 2023

All rights reserved. No part of this publication
may be produced, distributed, or transmitted in any form or by
any means, including photocopying, recording, or other electronic
or mechanical methods, without the prior written permission of
the publisher or except in the case of brief quotations embodied
in critical reviews and certain other non-commercial uses
permitted by copyright law.
For permission requests, write to the publisher, addressed:
"Attention: Permissions Coordinator" to Robert Jones
Published by Robert Jones

Cover Design & Layout by David Springer.

Contents

Introduction	Your True Kingdom Identity	7
Chapter 01	Your Kingship	17
Chapter 02	Your Ambassadorship	33
Chapter 03	Your Sonship	47
Chapter 04	Your Priesthood	59
Chapter 05	You Are The Body Of Christ	73
Chapter 06	The Bride Of Christ	87
Chapter 07	Your Kingdom Citizenship	99
Chapter 08	Your Discipleship	115
Chapter 09	How To Practically Start Walking In Your Kingdom Identity	127
Bonus Chapter	Christ's Identity Is Your Identity	141

YOUR TRUE KINGDOM

Identity

THE MAJESTY WITHIN

ROBERT JONES

Introduction

Your True Kingdom Identity

You Are Much More Than A Christian

Let me share with you a powerful key about your Kingdom identity. Many Believers struggle because they don't know who they are. For example, we have a label called Christian or Christianity. As you know, the Bible mentions the word Christian, three times.

Acts 11:26

And when he had found him, he brought him unto Antioch. And it came to pass, that a whole year they assembled themselves with the church, and taught much people. And the disciples were called Christians first in Antioch.

(This event took place in AD42, approximately 10 years after the Ascension of Jesus.)

Acts 26:28
Then Agrippa said unto Paul, Almost thou persuadest me to be a Christian.

(This event took place in AD62, approximately 30 years after the Ascension of Jesus.)

1 Peter 4:16
Yet if any man suffer as a Christian, let him not be ashamed; but let him glorify God on this behalf.

(This event took place in AD64, approximately 32 years after the Ascension of Jesus.)

The name Christian was a label or derogatory term that was coined by the unbelievers of Antioch, so that they could identify the disciples of this relatively new movement. What we need to understand is that the name Christian was never given to the Believers by Christ or The Apostles. It was used to mock the Believers. Now, the question you may be asking yourself is, why am I telling you all this? The reason is because I want to show you that the wealth of our Kingdom's new identity is not attached to the title, Christian. Also, the name Christian has obscured and hidden our Kingdom Identity.

As you know, the name Christian has been twisted, warped and infiltrated by the devil. Back in the time of Acts, the name Christian clearly identified the Book of Acts Believers, but today it does not. I live in the UK and supposedly, it's a Christian country just like the USA and Canada, but the UK is anything but Christ-like. So many people refer to themselves as Christians, but they are the biggest sinners around. The name Christian has been polluted by the 40,000 different denominations which have led to total disunity in the body of Christ. You have the Baptists who disagree with the Pentecostals and the Pentecostals disagree with the Anglicans, so on and so forth.

The name Christian means so many different things to different people. For some people, when they hear the name Christian, they automatically think about the Crusades which were a series of religious wars initiated, supported, and sometimes directed by the Latin Church in the mediaeval period.

For some cultures, the word Christian means a *White man's religion* with a *White man's God* that was forced onto weaker nations, and at the same time, erased that culture from off the face of the earth.

Have you ever heard of the slave bible which was forced upon the slaves who were shipped to the Americas from West Africa? Well, that slave bible only contained 232 chapters, while the full Bible contains 1,189 chapters.

Slave owners omitted 957 chapters which the Bible warns against.

Romans 1:18

For the wrath of God is revealed from heaven against all ungodliness and unrighteousness of men, who hold the truth in unrighteousness;

These slave owners were holding the truth back in unrighteousness by using the Word to manipulate their slaves to keep them subservient. The Catholics and even the Church of England, in times past, used the Bible to manipulate their parishioners on different levels, and became rich in the process. The point I'm trying to convey is that when you say the name Christian, these are some of the things which some people think about.

Mormons call themselves Christians even though many of their practices and what they believe are not even found in the 66 books of the Bible. Catholics, Jehovah's Witnesses and Seventh-day Adventists all call themselves Christians, even though their beliefs are so different in regards to what the other denominations believe. How can this be of God, as we all know God is not the author of confusion? If someone asked me if I was a Christian, I would say, yes, only so that they knew that I followed Jesus, but I would quickly switch it to a Kingdom conversation and begin to release the wealth of my Kingdom identity.

Understanding Our True Kingdom Identity

God wants you to understand your true identity, so while you're living here on the earth, doing the things of the Kingdom, you'll know who you are and how things work and operate. Without this understanding, you're not going to move in any victory. When you understand what is required of a king, an ambassador, a son of God, a Kingdom citizen, a priest, being the body of Christ, the bride and a disciple of Christ; you will see your life go to a new level. Being a son of God is different from us operating as an ambassador for Christ because of their distinct functions within the Kingdom.

Here in the UK, Prince Philip, Queen Elizabeth the second's husband, died in 2021. Prince Philip had the royal title of "The Queen's Consort". Those who are consorts of monarchs in the United Kingdom and its predecessors have no constitutional status or power, but many have had significant influence. Prince Philip, not only had the title of consort to the queen, he also had other titles. These are the names of some of his titles: The Duke of Edinburgh, Earl of Merioneth and Baron Greenwich, Knight of the Most Noble Order of the Garter, Knight of the Most Ancient and Most Noble Order of the Thistle. He also had numerous military titles.

His son, Prince Charles, before he became King, also had numerous titles. Here are just a few to give you a taste; Prince Charles, Prince of Wales, Duke of Cornwall,

Duke of Rothesay, Duke of Edinburgh, Earl of Chester, Earl of Carrick, Earl of Merioneth, Baron of Renfrew, Baron Greenwich, Lord of the Isles, Prince and Great Steward of Scotland. Each of these titles mean different things, and they all have different functions, authority and responsibilities. A duke is a lower rank under a prince and a knight is very different to a baron, but Prince Charles had the authority to operate in all of his titles.

Now, why am I telling you all of this? I do love history and the study of how kingdoms work, but I am setting you up for something BIG. Do you know that Jesus has bestowed upon the born-again Believer many titles, so that we can operate on different levels within the Kingdom of Heaven? We are kings; We are ambassadors; We are sons of God; We are Kingdom citizens; We are priests; we are the body of Christ; we are the bride of Christ and we are disciples. These are eight Kingdom titles we have because of Jesus, and each of these titles has a different function and operation.

When we understand what these titles and their different operations are and how they work, then we will live life on a different level. The devil doesn't want you to know this; he just wants you to be a good Christian who goes to church on a Sunday, and he doesn't mind that you read a few scriptures during the week. However, when you start to get the concept that you are a son of God, or that you are a part of a royal family; or when it begins to dawn on you that you are a king and you are also an ambassador or a Chief diplomatic officer who represents a Kingdom and its King, you will begin to see yourself differently. It's not enough to JUST see yourself as a Christian or a follower of Christ; we have to see ourselves according to what the Bible says.

The title of Christian, will always signify that you follow Jesus and you are part of a religion, or that you are a religious person that sings a few hymns and a few songs on a Sunday. It also suggests that you may pray for people, read the Bible here and there, or do your daily devotions by way of a Bible app. The devil doesn't want you to know that you have rights and privileges as a Kingdom citizen. We have to grasp this basic revelation that when we surrender our lives to Christ, we become so much more than simply a Christian.

Let's dive into some of the titles which the Bible calls us.

YOUR TRUE KINGDOM

Identity

THE MAJESTY WITHIN

CHAPTER #1

CHAPTER #1

Your Kingship

Wow, we are kings? Yes, and Jesus is the King of kings. Who is Jesus the King over? The answer is, US. You thought that the Bible was speaking about earthly kings. Even though God can override or use evil human rulers and leaders here on earth, the evil rulers and leaders do not refer to God as King. The Believers who are kings do refer to God as King. This is why He is the King of kings. You need to understand that kings are royal and kings rule over territories and kingdoms. What kingdom do we reign in, I hear you ask? Well, let's see what the Bible says:

2 Timothy 2:12
If we suffer, we shall also reign with him: if we deny him, he also will deny us:

Rev 1:6
And hath made us kings and priests unto God and his Father; to him be glory and dominion for ever and ever. Amen.

Rev 20:4

And I saw thrones, and they sat upon them, and judgment was given unto them: and I saw the souls of them that were beheaded for the witness of Jesus, and for the word of God, and which had not worshipped the beast, neither his image, neither had received his mark upon their foreheads, or in their hands; and they lived and reigned with Christ a thousand years.

Rev 22:5

And there shall be no night there; and they need no candle, neither light of the sun; for the Lord God giveth them light: and they shall reign for ever and ever

When are we kings? Well, we are kings right now. Remember, Adam was a king that ruled over the earth realm.

Gen 1:26

And God said, Let us make man in our image, after our likeness: and let them have dominion over the fish of the sea, and over the fowl of the air, and over the cattle, and over all the earth, and over every creeping thing that creepeth upon the earth.

The word *dominion* in the original Hebrew is "Rada", which basically means to have rule, have dominion, dominate and as you know, only kings and royalty can do this. God gave Adam a kingdom to rule over and that kingdom was the earth. It goes a little deeper than that because four other kingdoms also fell under Adams' jurisdiction. These kingdoms were the Animal, the Sea, the Air and the Creeping thing kingdoms.

God gave Adam the power and the authority to rule as the sovereign power on the earth, but as we all know, Satan coveted this power. He wanted it for himself and tricked Adam and Eve into rebelling against God, and in doing so, Adam lost his right to rule and reign. Adam lost Kingdom wealth. You may be asking what kingdom wealth Adam lost. Well, he lost his dominion and right to reign as a king. However, Jesus has restored this title back to those who believe in Him and have been born again.

How Do We Rule As Kings?

Well, this is a very powerful question and to answer it, we first have to go to a specific scripture to get the context of our rulership.

Ephesian 2:6

And hath raised us up together, and made us sit together in heavenly places in Christ Jesus:

The first thing we have to comprehend is that we are seated with Christ at the right hand of God. There aren't two Thrones in Heaven, even though the Bible says that Jesus is seated on the right hand of the Father in Heaven. That, there, is what is called a Hebrew idiom. So basically, whenever someone is seated on the right hand, it means they are seated in the place of power. We see this with Jacob's son, Benjamin; Benjamin means the son of my power, or the son of my strength. Jacob's power was in his son in the same way that the Father's power is committed to the Son. In other words, Jesus is the power of God.

1 Corinthians 1:24

But unto them which are called, both Jews and Greeks, Christ the power of God, and the wisdom of God.

Another thing we must understand about Kings is that they are always seated on their thrones. Kings do not stand as their citizens or subjects stand, waiting to promptly execute commands.

1 Kings 22:19

And he said, Hear thou therefore the word of the Lord: I saw the Lord sitting on his throne, and all the host of heaven standing by him on his right hand and on his left.

Daniel 7:10

A fiery stream issued and came forth from before him: thousand thousands ministered unto him, and ten thousand times ten thousand stood before him: the judgment was set, and the books were opened.

Revelation 7:11

And all the angels stood round about the throne, and about the elders and the four beasts, and fell before the throne on their faces, and worshipped God,

Here are a few Scriptures of God seated on His throne.

Psalms 47:8

God reigneth over the heathen: God sitteth upon the throne of his holiness.

Isaiah 6:1

In the year that king Uzziah died I saw also the Lord sitting upon a throne, high and lifted up, and his train filled the temple.

Daniel 7:9

I beheld till the thrones were cast down, and the Ancient of days did sit, whose garment was white as snow, and the hair of his head like the pure wool: his throne was like the fiery flame, and his wheels as burning fire.

Revelation 4:10

The four and twenty elders fall down before him that sat on the throne, and worship him that liveth for ever and ever, and cast their crowns before the throne, saying,

Revelation 20:11

And I saw a great white throne, and him that sat on it, from whose face the earth and the heaven fled away; and there was found no place for them.

Kings don't work, they give orders and commands and they must be carried out; this is the authority a king has. Kings speak and it is done, it's that simple. No one can argue and no one can disagree with the king's commands and orders. We, as Believers, have this same power because we are seated with Christ in heavenly places, and we know that Jesus is seated in the place of All Power.

To be able to move in this type of power and authority, we have to be spiritual. We have to be spiritual to remain seated. If we are carnal, then we will be standing and working to get things done in our own strength. We will be standing with the angels that are about God's throne, waiting to do His commands, instead of being seated with Christ giving the commands that are in alignment with the will of God.

Psalms 103:20
Bless the LORD, ye his angels, that excel in strength, that do his commandments, hearkening unto the voice of his word.

Remember, there's nowhere in the Bible where angels are called kings, nor are they ever in a position to give commands like a king. Angels receive and execute the commands given by God, seated on His throne. The only angel that was called a king in the Bible is the devil, but he is an illegal king that usurped his authority from Adam.

How To Move In Rulership

You can only rule in and over your life from above; you have to rule from a heavenly place. You have to see things from a spiritual or heavenly perspective. Let me give you an example:

Psalms 2:1-4

Why do the heathen rage, and the people imagine a vain thing?

The kings of the earth set themselves, and the rulers take counsel together, against the LORD, and against his anointed, saying,

Let us break their bands asunder, and cast away their cords from us.

He that sitteth in the heavens shall laugh: the Lord shall have them in derision.

You see, for the heathens, from an earthly perspective their plan made sense, but from a heavenly perspective their plan was futile, and God was laughing at them. It's the same with us; from an earthly perspective the bank is going to foreclose or repossess your house, or the doctors have given you an unfavourable diagnosis. But when you see these situations from a heavenly perspective, you will laugh because you are seated as a king and you have the power to reverse these decisions.

The caveat is that you have to remain spiritual or the situations of life will overwhelm you, and you will look for earthly solutions to your earthly situation, when you can simply stay seated with Christ and command this situation to be reversed in the name of Jesus. Interestingly, Jesus shows us how to move as a king; He is our template. Jesus was called the 'King of the Jews' when He was here on the earth 2000 years ago, and what did we see Him do? We saw Him give commands and orders just like a king.

The Word Of A King

Let me show you a powerful scripture about Kings.

Ecclesiastes 8:4

Where the word of a king is, there is power: and who may say unto him, What doest thou?

The word of a king is truly powerful. When a king speaks, everyone takes heed because the king is the ultimate authority in a kingdom, and his word is law. This is the same for earthly kings and God as King. The best way to understand the power of a king is to study the kings of Israel and even the heathen kings mentioned in the Bible, like Nebuchadnezzar and Cyrus, king of the Meads and Persians. These kings had power to change the direction or laws of their kingdoms, from the far left to the far right with just one word.

Cyrus, king of Persia, in the Book of Ezra, freed Judah from captivity. Not only did he free them, he also gave a command that they were allowed to rebuild the wall and temple at Jerusalem, and he gave them all the resources they needed to get it done.

King Manasseh in 2 Kings 21, was also an evil king who ruled over Judah for 55 years, and he led Judah into idol worship and the serving of devils. When he died, his son Amon ruled, and he was just as evil as his father, Manasseh. When Amon died, his son Josiah ruled. Josiah was a good king and he had the power and authority to turn Judah 180 degrees into the opposite direction, from serving devils to serving God.

Now, when we look at God, it's the same thing; the power of His words is far greater than that of earthly kings'. Here is the secret; the Believer also has this awesome kingly power. We have to be in sync with Jesus the same way He was in sync with the Father, i.e. Jesus only did and said what He saw and heard His father doing and saying.

John 5:19
Then answered Jesus and said unto them, Verily, verily, I say unto you, The Son can do nothing of himself, but what he seeth the Father do: for what things soever he doeth, these also doeth the Son likewise.

John 12:49

For I have not spoken of myself; but the Father which sent me, he gave me a commandment, what I should say, and what I should speak.

In Christ's ministry, Jesus was in perfect sync with His father so much so that He only said and did what He saw His father saying and doing. Jesus is the template, and we are supposed to do what He did. Now, don't get me wrong, I do realise that Jesus was perfect and we are not, but we do have something to aim at.

Our desires, thoughts, will, etc., have to become God's. In other words, we should only do and say what God is doing and saying, and our desires and will need to be in alignment with God's. When we begin to live this way, where, what we say, think and do, is what God thinks, says and does, then whatever we say or command will come to pass because it's what God has commanded.

This is a powerful revelation because now you can begin to understand why, when a Believer commands or decrees something like a king, nothing happens. The reason nothing happens for the most part, is because what we are commanding or decreeing is not in alignment with the mind of the King of our country, which is Heaven. So there is no reason to get upset or frustrated when your prayers don't get answered, because you now know the answer. You need to ask yourself this, *is what I'm saying aligned with what is being said in Heaven?*

If We Are Kings, Then What Do We Rule Over?

We Get to rule within the gifts that God has given to us and there are many which are mentioned in the Bible, and many which are not.

Apostles, Prophets, Evangelists, Pastors and Teachers are gifts; they are also very important offices within the Church that only a minority of the Church have been called to operate in. We are very aware of the nine gifts of the Holy Spirit which are; wisdom, knowledge, faith, gifts of healing, the working of miracles, prophecy, discerning of spirits, diverse kinds of tongues and the interpretation of tongues.

Did you know that the Holy Spirit is also a gift that was given to us by God? And because we have the Holy Spirit, we have the ability to operate in other gifts as well. Let me share a few more with you; grace is a gift and so is salvation and Justification; eternal life and understanding mysteries. Christ is a gift, and all perfect gifts come from God. Let's not forget about the gift of helps and governments as without these gifts in operation, the Church would cease to function properly.

These are just a few of the gifts which are mentioned in the Bible, but I would also like to mention one other; the gift of giving. There are many in the body of Christ who struggle to give, whether it's their time, talent or treasure, to the furthering of Kingdom work in the earth. There are things which are very simple for you to do and some find it hard, and they wonder how you can do it so effortlessly. Well, for a Believer, that's a gift from God and it must be used to further Kingdom business. Don't sit on that gift or talent because they will lay dormant, and you will be bypassed and the one who is willing, will receive the benefits or resources of using their gift or talent .

We are a Kingdom of kings, and Jesus is the King of kings. We do not rule over each other, but we rule within the kingdom that God has given to us. We get our concept of kings ruling over people from the world, but we do not rule that way. The concept of rulership for us as kings, is very different from that of the world. Man ruling over other men is a fallen concept. Adam was the first earth king.

When Eve, or the woman was created, Adam did not rule over her even though he was a king. Adam was given specific things that he had dominion over and it was not his wife. However, after the fall, you see Adam given rule over his wife and then, after that, you start seeing people rising up in the earth dominating and subjugating other humans. This was not God's original plan. Jesus rules over us and we rule in the Kingdom that He has given us to rule over, or within.

When we understand that we are a Kingdom of kings, and we get the revelation of our royalty, then the search is on for us to find the kingdom we have been given to rule over, and like I said earlier, it's not over people. The kingdom that you have been given to rule over is referring to the gifts and skills which God has given to you. When you become the king of your thing, then there is no need for me to compete with you or vice versa.

You see, because I know what gifts, talents and skills God has given to me at present, I am not intimidated by anyone's unique gifts, and I do not need to covet what they have. I celebrate them and I celebrate them when they are promoted by God and granted more gifts and skills. We are all kings with unique callings on our lives, this is why the Bible says;

2 Corinthians 10:12

For we dare not make ourselves of the number, or compare ourselves with some that commend themselves: but they measuring themselves by themselves, and comparing themselves among themselves, are not wise.

We shouldn't covet other Believers' gifts, achievements or try to emulate them, because they are not the standard of living. Jesus is our standard and He is the one we should seek to emulate and mould ourselves after, not some top level Prophet, Apostle or Preacher.

YOUR TRUE KINGDOM

Identity

THE MAJESTY WITHIN

CHAPTER #2

CHAPTER #2

Your Ambassadorship

What Is An Ambassador?

An ambassador is a high-ranking diplomat who represents a sovereign state, an international organisation or their own government. He or she is appointed for a special and often temporary, diplomatic assignment. Death Or Rapture = End Of Assignment.

Top diplomatic officers have full immunity, as do their deputies and families. This means ambassadors can commit just about any crime—from jaywalking, to murder—and still be immune from prosecution. They can't be arrested or forced to testify in court.

An ambassador is a spokesperson for a country, a spokesperson for an organisation, or a spokesperson for a corporation or a business. Ambassadors speak on behalf of the place that they are representing.

The Bible says that born-again Believers are ambassadors for Christ.

2 Corinthians 5:20
Now then we are ambassadors for Christ, as though God did beseech you by us: we pray you in Christ's stead, be ye reconciled to God.

Ephesians 6:20
For which I am an ambassador in bonds: that therein I may speak boldly, as I ought to speak.

One of the things we must understand is that the role of an ambassador is temporary.

We Are Ambassadors for Christ, and one of the most important things we must remember is that neither a king nor an ambassador is a religion. A King is a ruler over a country, and an Ambassador is a diplomat sent from a country to be a spokesperson and representative of that country in a foreign territory. When you say that you're a Christian, people think of religion; but when you say that you're an ambassador, now you're speaking a governmental language. Like I said earlier, an ambassador is not a religion. As Believers, we should know that Jesus did not bring a religion, He brought a kingdom.

This part is very important and many Believers do not understand or have not been exposed to the fact that Heaven is an actual country that has a King, Laws and Citizens. The more you understand this revelation, the more you will begin to change. Jesus tells us over and over in the Bible that He was not from the earth, but rather from a different place or country.

The Kingdom of Heaven is a country, it's a land, it's a territory, a realm in a different dimension which God Rules over.

John 3:13
And no man hath ascended up to heaven, but he that came down from heaven, even the Son of man which is in heaven.

John 6:38
For I came down from heaven, not to do mine own will, but the will of him that sent me.

John 6:51
I am the living bread which came down from heaven: if any man eat of this bread, he shall live for ever: and the bread that I will give is my flesh, which I will give for the life of the world.

John 8:23
And he said unto them, Ye are from beneath; I am from above: ye are of this world; I am not of this world.

John 18:36

Jesus answered, My kingdom is not of this world: if my kingdom were of this world, then would my servants fight, that I should not be delivered to the Jews: but now is my kingdom not from hence.

Throughout Jesus' ministry, He constantly said that He was from another place, and that place was Heaven. In essence, Jesus was not only a King and a Son, He was also an Ambassador because He was a representative and a spokesperson for Heaven. As Believers, we also have the title of Ambassadors laid upon us. As the ambassadors of the Kingdom of Heaven (which is a country), it is Heaven's responsibility to fully resource its ambassadors.

When we are doing what we are supposed to do, Heaven will ensure that we receive everything we need so that we can carry out our assignment on Earth. We can enjoy everything Heaven has to offer as long as we stay in alignment with its King. If we move out of alignment with the King of Heaven, then the resources will stop flowing to us.

Did you know that as ambassadors, we have diplomatic immunity through the blood of Jesus? This means the accuser can no longer have a hold on us unless we step outside of the bounds of our assignment and act like the world.

James 4:4

Ye adulterers and adulteresses, know ye not that the friendship of the world is enmity with God? whosoever therefore will be a friend of the world is the enemy of God.

1 John 2:15-16

Love not the world, neither the things that are in the world. If any man love the world, the love of the Father is not in him.

For all that is in the world, the lust of the flesh, and the lust of the eyes, and the pride of life, is not of the Father, but is of the world.

So, acting like the world, cuts off your heavenly supply. We need to bear in mind that Satan is always trying to tempt us to go against what our King says, because he knows that if we do, then Heaven's resources will be cut off from us; not because God cuts the supply, but because we have come out of alignment with the Kingdom that we represent as ambassadors. The Apostle John reveals to us in *1 John 2:16* that Satan only temps mankind in three areas:

1 John 2:16

For all that is in the world, the lust of the flesh, and the lust of the eyes, and the pride of life, is not of the Father, but is of the world.

1# The lust of the flesh / Physical Desires

Now the lust of the flesh is fleshly appetites. If we are led by the flesh in the pursuit of fleshly pleasures, we will come up against God and we will lose. Galatians 5:19-21 gives a long list of fleshly desires that must be avoided:

Galatians 5:19-21
Now the works of the flesh are manifest, which are these; Adultery, fornication, uncleanness, lasciviousness, Idolatry, witchcraft,
hatred, variance, emulations, wrath, strife, seditions, heresies,

Envyings, murders, drunkenness, revellings, and such like: of the which I tell you before, as I have also told you in time past, that they which do such things shall not inherit the kingdom of God.

These are also called unrighteous lifestyles or the culture of the kingdom of darkness. I cover this in greater detail in my book called, The Kingdom Hand Book.

2# The lust of the eyes / Personal Desires

These are personal desires or desires to obtain and possess things that look good to the eyes. The love of money is at the top of the list and second would be coveting physical things which are not from God, but are from the world. There is nothing wrong with you desiring a house, a spouse, new clothes, a car, a promotion at work, a degree, etc. I'm speaking about the lust of the eyes where your desire or desires are rampant and out of control.

When your desires are rampant and out of control, they will lead you into envy and jealousy. When you become envious and jealous, you will be led into sin and bondage by the devil. Jealousy is when you want what someone has or covet someone else's possessions. Envy is when you are jealous of someone else's possessions but you don't want them to have them either.

Having an evil desire to obtain and possess all the things that we see, or having an unrighteous desire to acquire all the things that are appealing to the eyes, are not from God. This also applies to coveting possessions, money, or anything that the world has to offer. The Holy Spirit reveals to us through the Apostle John's epistle, that physical things do not last and they will ultimately fade away. This is the same thing that Jesus taught in His ministry that we must build up treasure in Heaven for they are eternal, but the things on the earth are temporal.

3# The Pride of life / Self Interests

The pride of life can be seen as anything that is of the world or anything that leads you to exaggerate your own worth or importance. The pride of life is the total opposite of being humble, and we know from the scriptures that God resists proud and arrogant people.

Satanic Ambassadors

James 4:6

But he giveth more grace. Wherefore he saith, God resisteth the proud, but giveth grace unto the humble.

2 Corinthians 5:20 states that we are Ambassadors for Christ, BUT Satan also has his ambassadors with a fallen message, and they represent a fallen king and kingdom.

Any person, Government or Industry that promotes the scriptures below, are Ambassadors that represent the kingdom of darkness. Remember that an ambassador is a spokesperson of a kingdom, but in this case, the kingdom of darkness.

Gal 5:19-21

Now the works of the flesh are manifest, which are these; Adultery, fornication, uncleanness, lasciviousness,

Idolatry, witchcraft, hatred, variance, emulations, wrath, strife, seditions, heresies,

Envyings, murders, drunkenness, revellings, and such like: of the which I tell you before, as I have also told you in time past, that they which do such things shall not inherit the kingdom of God.

1 Cor 6:9-10
Know ye not that the unrighteous shall not inherit the kingdom of God? Be not deceived: neither fornicators, nor idolaters, nor adulterers, nor effeminate, nor abusers of themselves with mankind,

Nor thieves, nor covetous, nor drunkards, nor revilers, nor extortioners, shall inherit the kingdom of God.

Satan and his angels are fallen ambassadors with a fallen message. Adam was an ambassador representing the King of Heaven on Earth. As we know, when he sinned, he handed over his Dominion and kingship to Satan. Jesus, as a man, was a Kingdom Ambassador because He spoke on behalf of The King.

John 12:49-50
For I have not spoken of myself; but the Father which sent me, he gave me a commandment, what I should say, and what I should speak.

And I know that his commandment is life everlasting: whatsoever I speak therefore, even as the Father said unto me, so I speak.

John 5:19-20

Then answered Jesus and said unto them, Verily, verily, I say unto you, The Son can do nothing of himself, but what he seeth the Father do: for what things soever he doeth, these also doeth the Son likewise.

For the Father loveth the Son, and sheweth him all things that himself doeth: and he will shew him greater works than these, that ye may marvel.

Many of the world's celebrities, social media influencers, musicians, politicians, etc, are what I call "pastors or apostles of darkness". This is because all they do is promote a fallen message from a dark kingdom. They spread darkness amongst those they have influence over. The same way God uses the Believers to spread the Kingdom's message of light and freedom in Jesus, is the same way they spread the message of death and destruction. The sad thing is for the most part, these apostles and pastors of darkness have been deceived by the dark message they spread.

Who Is The Head Of The Ambassadors?

This is a very easy question to answer. The Holy Spirit is the head of all of the ambassadors on the earth. When I say ambassadors, I am speaking about those who come under the Lordship of Jesus Christ. The Holy Spirit is like the Secretary of State; all of the country's ambassadors report to the Secretary of State. The Secretary of State has direct contact with the president, prime minister, king or leader of that country. The Secretary of State knows what is on the mind of the head of that country, and it's their job to relay that information to the ambassadors.

1 Corinthians 2:10-11

But God hath revealed them unto us by his Spirit: for the Spirit searcheth all things, yea, the deep things of God.

For what man knoweth the things of a man, save the spirit of man which is in him? even so the things of God knoweth no man, but the Spirit of God.

According to this Scripture, the Holy Spirit is the only person who knows what God is thinking, as He is the only one who can search or know the deep things of God. The Holy Spirit is the Spirit of God and the Holy Spirit knows what is on the mind of God.

John 16:13

Howbeit when he, the Spirit of truth, is come, he will guide you into all truth: for he shall not speak of himself; but whatsoever he shall hear, that shall he speak: and he will shew you things to come.

The Holy Spirit is the one who leads us into all truth, which is a little bit of a paradox because Jesus is the Truth, so ultimately, the Holy Spirit leads us to Jesus. As the Ambassadors of Christ, we have to be in contact with the Holy Spirit so that we can be kept up to date with what the King wants us to do. This is why prayer and fellowship with the Holy Spirit is so important. I do know that what I've said can lead to many questions about the Godhead, but I was just trying to explain it in the simplest way I could.

One thing we must recognize however, is that the Holy Spirit plays a Big part in us understanding the will and plans of the King of our country.

YOUR TRUE KINGDOM

Identity

THE MAJESTY WITHIN

CHAPTER #3

CHAPTER #3

Your Sonship

Being a son of God links us to divinity or God likeness. God is a Spirit and God is a King and we are His sons. So, if we are His sons, that means we are a part of a royal family. Christianity and a royal family are not the same, as one is connected to a religion and the other is not. We are not part of a religion, but part of a royal family. This is what the Bible is really talking about: A King, His Kingdom and His royal family.

I want to show you two very powerful verses in the Bible that reveal to us God's royalty.

Genesis 1:1
In the beginning God created the heaven and the earth.

Isaiah 66:1
Thus saith the LORD, The heaven is my throne, and the earth is my footstool: where is the house that ye build unto me? and where is the place of my rest?

These two Scriptures are absolutely packed with revelation. Isaiah and many other verses throughout the Bible, teaches that Heaven is God's throne and Earth is His footstool. In Genesis 1:1, it states that God created the Heaven and the Earth. So, God first created a throne, i.e. Heaven and then a footstool, i.e. Earth. I want to point out that only Kings sit on thrones and rest their feet on footstools. The first thing that God reveals to us is that He is God or the Supreme Being. Then He reveals Himself to us as a King who rules over a Kingdom. Armed with this revelation, let's look at Genesis 1:1 again.

Genesis 1:1

In the beginning (the Supreme Being) created a (Throne) and a (Footstool).

There are so many other revelations that are hidden in the first verse of revelation that would make your head spin, but those revelations are outside the scope of this book.

God's Royal Family

We know that the angels were the first sons of God, and they first appear in chronological order at the laying of the foundations of the earth. In the Old Testament, when you see a reference to "the sons of God", it is always referring to Angels or the "Bene-elohim" in the Hebrew, if you want to get deep.

Job 38:6-7

Whereupon are the foundations thereof fastened? or who laid the corner stone thereof;

When the morning stars sang together, and all the sons of God shouted for joy?

This Scripture is referring to a time when there was harmony and unity in Heaven. It teaches that all of the sons of God, including Lucifer who the Bible calls a morning star (Isa 14:12), were shouting for Joy. Foolishly, many of these angelic sons of God rebelled against the Sovereign King of Heaven, and in doing so, they lost their relationship with God and all the privileges of sonship. They are no longer classed as royalty holding a high office, they are now the scourge of mankind. When we see Satan appear in front of God in the Book of Job chapters one and two, and study the conversation between God and Satan, there is no relationship between the two, even though Job 1:6 still calls Satan a son of God. Angels are called sons of God, the good ones and the bad ones.

Originally, God created man in His own Image and after His own likeness.

Genesis 1:26

And God said, Let us make man in our image, after our likeness: and let them have dominion over the fish of the sea, and over the fowl of the air, and over the cattle, and over all the earth, and over every creeping thing that creepeth upon the earth.

God is a King, and Adam was made in His likeness. Remember that God's likeness is kingly and royal, amongst other things. Adam was made in the likeness of The King, and kings rule over territory, and the territory that Adam was given to rule over was the kingdom of the earth. Adam was supposed to rule over the earth from his kingdom headquarters, the garden of Eden. Through the creation of Adam, God added mankind to His royal family. It was God's original plan to have a royal family, but as we all know, Adam failed in this task and lost everything. It was a very sad day. When Adam sinned, he lost so many things and one of them was his sonship, or his loss of relationship with the Father. No relationship with the Father means no connection with royalty. Even though Adam was still called a son of God *(Luke 3:38)*, just like the angels who rebelled against God, he no longer had access to the privileges that sonship has to offer.

Restoration

God's plan has always been to restore man to the place where he fell from. The Apostle Paul reveals to us through the revelation of the Holy Spirit, the ministry of reconciliation or being restored back to a position of royalty.

2 Corinthians 5:18-19

And all things [are] of God, who hath reconciled us to himself by Jesus Christ, and hath given to us the ministry of reconciliation;

To wit, that God was in Christ, reconciling the world unto himself, not imputing their trespasses unto them; and hath committed unto us the word of reconciliation.

Ephesians 2:16

And that he might reconcile both unto God in one body by the cross, having slain the enmity thereby:

Colosians 1:20

And, having made peace through the blood of his cross, by him to reconcile all things unto himself; by him, [I say], whether [they be] things in earth, or things in heaven.

God has an original plan that is laid out in Genesis 1:26 and that plan is for man to be a king over the earth realm. Remember, the Bible is about a King, His Kingdom and His royal family. It doesn't matter what happens, everything will end up back to how God intended it to be originally. We see the fulfilment of God's original plan in Revelation chapters 21 and 22, with a new heaven and a new earth.

Why Did Jesus Come To The Earth?

Now we have been armed with the understanding of the ministry of reconciliation, we can better understand why Jesus is so powerful. Jesus was the only one who could come to the earth and restore our relationship with the Father by restoring our sonship. By the death, burial and resurrection of Jesus, the born again Believers are now called the Sons of God.

John 1:12

But as many as received him, to them gave he power to become the sons of God, even to them that believe on his name:

Romans 8:14

For as many as are led by the Spirit of God, they are the sons of God.

Romans 8:19

For the earnest expectation of the creature waiteth for the manifestation of the sons of God.

Philippians 2:15

That ye may be blameless and harmless, the sons of God, without rebuke, in the midst of a crooked and perverse nation, among whom ye shine as lights in the world;

1 John 3:1-2

Behold, what manner of love the Father hath bestowed upon us, that we should be called the sons of God: therefore the world knoweth us not, because it knew him not.

Beloved, now are we the sons of God, and it doth not yet appear what we shall be: but we know that, when he shall appear, we shall be like him; for we shall see him as he is.

Sonship is a very powerful thing that Jesus restored to those who follow Him. Now, the Believers are also the sons of God and we are treated by God as such. Sons are granted favour, kindness, grace, love, acceptance, mercy, access and so many other privileges. We are given all of the things that an earthly father would give to his son, just to bring a little bit of context. Obviously, we cannot compare our heavenly Father to our earthly one.

Misunderstood Verses That Satan Uses To Attack the Believer

There are a few verses in scripture which the devil likes to twist, or weaponize and attack the Believers with, like "Blasphemy of the Holy Spirit" and the verses below that we are about to explore. These attacks only work when the Believer is ignorant of what the scriptures mean.

Matthew 7:22-23

Many will say to me in that day, Lord, Lord, have we not prophesied in thy name? and in thy name have cast out devils? and in thy name done many wonderful works?

And then will I profess unto them, I never knew you: depart from me, ye that work iniquity.

Now, this is a massive question in the minds of so many Believers, and for the most part, they don't have an answer for it and they live in a place of uncertainty and continuous searching. The devil has put so much fear into some Believers, that they think they will be the ones who Jesus is speaking about. Jesus is speaking about those who did signs and wonders in His name, but at some point in their walk, they turned back.

Luke 9:62

And Jesus said unto him, No man, having put his hand to the plough, and looking back, is fit for the kingdom of God.

There were many disciples that turned away from Jesus, even though they did many things in His name like Judas, and I also suspect many of the 70 disciples that Jesus sent out to preach the Kingdom in Luke 10:1. The Bible even teaches in John 6:51-52 that when Jesus proclaimed to be the Bread of Life, everyone had to eat His flesh and drink His blood to be able to receive everlasting life. At the end of this revelation that Jesus was sharing, the Bible shows us the response of many of his disciples.

John 6:66
From that time many of his disciples went back, and walked no more with him.

When you turn your back on Jesus, you lose your sonship and relationship with the Father. These are the ones to whom Jesus will say, "I never knew you". If you are following and believing in Jesus, then your sonship and relationship with the Father is intact, so you have nothing to worry about.

Here is another verse that many Believers think is aimed at the Church, but this cannot be further from the truth.

Matthew 8:12
But the children of the kingdom shall be cast out into outer darkness: there shall be weeping and gnashing of teeth.

The 'children of the Kingdom' that is mentioned in this verse, are the children of Israel. The Kingdom and salvation was promised to them first, but they rejected Jesus, and in doing so, the Kingdom has been given to others, i.e. anyone who accepts Jesus as Lord.

John 1:11-12

He came unto his own (Hebrews)*, and his own* (Hebrews) *received him not.*

But as many as received him, to them gave he power to become the sons of God, even to them that believe on his name:

The devil wants us to believe that no matter what we do, it will never be good enough to get into Heaven, but when we have the revelation of sonship, we will be free from this attack forever. We need to understand that entry into the Kingdom of God has nothing to do with us and everything to do with the finished works of Christ. Jesus was the one who restored our sonship and broke down the wall of partition that separated us from the Father.

YOUR TRUE KINGDOM

Identity

THE MAJESTY WITHIN

CHAPTER #4

CHAPTER #4

Your Priesthood

As Priests, we are mediators; we speak on behalf of the people. We are intercessors, we are an intermediary. In the Old Testament, the priest would go into the temple to sacrifice lambs, rams, birds, etc., for the sins of the people and for the sins of the nation. Christ is our High Priest and the Bible makes this very clear in the Scriptures below:

Hebrews 4:14

Seeing then that we have a great high priest, that is passed into the heavens, Jesus the Son of God, let us hold fast our profession.

1 Tim 2:5

For there is one God, and one mediator between God and men, the man Christ Jesus;

John 14:6

Jesus saith unto him, I am the way, the truth, and the life: no man cometh unto the Father, but by me.

Christ is saying, *I'm the intermediary, I'm the one in between, I'm the Priest.* We don't get to God without going through Christ, He is the door. What you need to understand is that we are the exact same thing on Earth. What I'm about to say next is a bit deep, so please, listen carefully. We are priests and no one can get to Christ but by us. What I've just said may be hard for some to comprehend, but let me explain. When you gave your life to Christ, did you just wander into a church and get saved? Did you just decide out of the blue to get saved? The answer is probably, No.

When God was working on your heart, you sought out those who went to church and those who you knew were saved, so that you could find out more about Jesus and eventually, get saved. The Believers you sought were priests or the intermediaries between Christ and you, although Jesus (who is the mediator between God and man) was the one who got you saved. I'm not speaking about Catholicism where people pray to Mary, then Mary prays to Jesus and Jesus prays to God. I'm speaking about how God uses Believers in the role of a Priest to intercede, pray and lead people to the Cross. This has happened to me many times throughout my walk with Christ. I have had family members, work colleagues and friends who asked me to tell them about the Lord.

The Apostle Paul said it in Romans;

Romans 10:14-15

How then shall they call on him in whom they have not believed? and how shall they believe in him of whom they have not heard? and how shall they hear without a preacher?

And how shall they preach, except they be sent? as it is written, How beautiful are the feet of them that preach the gospel of peace, and bring glad tidings of good things!

When the Apostle Paul was in his ministry, he led many to Christ. He not only led them, he also fed them the Word and prayed and interceded for them. This is the same thing that the Priests and the Levites did in the Old Testament. We know that the Levites were the priestly tribe and they were the ones whose function was to handle the holy things, to feed the people spiritual truths and stand in the gap for the children of Israel. This is exactly what all Believers have been called to do, i.e., the role of a Priest.

Jesus did this exact same thing. He handled holy things like the Holy Spirit which was in Him; He fed the people spiritual truths like the revelation of the Kingdom of God, and He stood in the gap for the people of the world by dying on the Cross. When the 120 came out of the upper room in Acts chapter two, Peter started to preach Christ, and at the end of his short sermon, the people who were seeking God, as they were in Jerusalem for the feast of Pentecost, asked Peter, "What shall we do?" and Peter, a New Testament priest, led them to Jesus because that is what Priests do; they lead people in the ways of righteousness.

A priest is sanctified and set apart for the Master's use. They are consecrated; priests are not defiled; priests live holy lives, and because priests live holy lives, they start to move with the holy things and the things of the Spirit. When priests move in the ways I've just mentioned, they start to get insights into the spirit world.

In the Bible, there were many priests who had dual callings; they were not only primarily priests, but they also had a prophetic calling on their lives. Samuel, Isaiah, Jeremiah, Ezekiel and Zechariah were all priests with a prophetic mantle. What is quite interesting, is that in the Old Testament, Isaiah, Jeremiah and Ezekiel were regarded as Major prophets because they had the largest amounts of prophecies, and they had longer books. Out of the minor prophets, with the exception of Hosea, Zechariah has fourteen chapters, while the other minor prophets have less. Even Samuel has two books named after him.

Samuel the prophet was very special because he was not only a priest and a prophet, but he was also the last Judge over Israel. Samuel was the one who closed the era of the judges and ushered in the era of the prophets.

Just to add a side note, John the Baptist was also a very special biblical character, because he was the last Old Testament priest who was also the prophet that prepared the way for the King of the Kingdom. Now, you can begin to understand why they were such great prophets. To be a priest, you had to live a certain lifestyle or you would lose your office. Priests had to be sanctified, Holy, passionate for the things of God and live very moral lives, or they would be rejected.

Now, this part is very important because if you don't understand your priesthood and that you're a priest, how are you going to move in the things of the Spirit? How are you going to move in spiritual gifts? How are you going to experience the fruit of the Spirit in your life? We can learn and read about spiritual things, but we will never experience them if we live unholy and immoral lifestyles.

You can't prophesy if your vessel is not sanctified and clean because you will not be able to hear God properly. Obviously, no one is perfect, and we all have challenges and issues, but some of us make poor choices and the fruit of those choices block up our spirit and God's ability to use us because we are out of alignment with Him.

When we read about prophets in the Old Testament like Daniel for example, he had an excellent spirit. He fasted regularly, he was a man of prayer and he did not defile himself; just to point out a few things in regard to his lifestyle. As you know, he was a powerful prophet who saw the future. Not only did he see the future, he also saw God, spoke to angels, interpreted dreams and he was one of the main rulers in Babylon and the Persian empires. You have probably experienced that when you were on fire for God and living a spiritually disciplined life. You were moving in so many giftings, or your spiritual senses went into overdrive, why? Well, that is because you were living according to priestly principles.

In the Old Testament, the first time the word 'priest' was mentioned was in

Genesis 14:18

And Melchizedek king of Salem brought forth bread and wine: and he [was] the priest of the most high God.

Melchizedek was a very interesting character and there have been many different theories of who he was. Some have said that Melchizedek was actually a pre-incarnate appearance of Jesus Christ, or a Christophany. Some have even suggested that Melchizedek was Shem, the first born of Noah, but the main thing I want to draw your attention to is that Melchizedek was a Priest and a King at the same time. According to Hebrews, Jesus is our High Priest after the order of Melchizedek

Hebrews 6:20

Whither the forerunner is for us entered, even Jesus, made an high priest for ever after the order of Melchisedec.

This means that Jesus is a King and a Priest just like Melchizedek in the Book of Genesis. This is where it gets very interesting because the Believers are also after the order of Melchizedek. The Bible calls us Kings and Priests.

Rev 1:6
And hath made us kings and priests unto God and his Father; to him be glory and dominion for ever and ever. Amen.

Rev 5:10
And hast made us unto our God kings and priests: and we shall reign on the earth.

Revelation 20:6
Blessed and holy is he that hath part in the first resurrection: on such the second death hath no power, but they shall be priests of God and of Christ, and shall reign with him a thousand years.

The Change Of Priesthood

Being a priest after the order of Melchizedek is such a powerful thing when you understand the gravity of "the changing of the priesthood". The first time we see Melchizedek who was a king and a priest at the same time, was in the book of Genesis *14:18*

Genesis 14:18
And Melchizedek king of Salem brought forth bread and wine: and he [was] the priest of the most high God.

Melchizedek met Abraham after the battle of the kings, and he brought bread and wine which, interestingly, are the Communion elements which represent Christ's body and blood, or the new covenant.

Genesis 14:20 goes on to say that Abraham gave him tithes of all he had, and in exchange for that, the Melchizedek priesthood was given to Abraham as it was his seed that would have exclusivity to God. Through Abraham's seed, you'll see the split of the kingship and priesthood of Melchizedek. The kingly line passed to Judah and the priestly line passed to Levi. Now all Jesus needed was the Priesthood to be given to Him so that He could restore the Melchizedek priesthood of King and Priest.

We know that Jesus was called the "King of the Jews", and to be the "King of the Jews", you have to be from the tribe of Judah. The Gospels of Matthew and Luke reveal that Christ was from the tribe of Judah through His mother Mary and (adoption through) His stepfather Joseph. With the death, burial and resurrection of Jesus, the Melchizedek priesthood was ultimately unified once again, under Christ.

The Priesthood Ripped From Levi

When Jesus was arrested in the Garden of Gethsemane, He was taken to the private residence of Caiaphas, the high priest, where the chief priests and elders tried to raise false witnesses against Jesus, but they couldn't find any. Eventually, they found two who witnessed against Jesus, but Jesus held His peace. Caiaphas then asked Jesus if He was going to defend Himself against the two witnesses, and if He was the Christ, the Son of God.

Matthew 26:64-66

Jesus saith unto him, Thou hast said: nevertheless I say unto you, Hereafter shall ye see the Son of man sitting on the right hand of power, and coming in the clouds of heaven.

Then the high priest rent his clothes, saying, He hath spoken blasphemy; what further need have we of witnesses? behold, now ye have heard his blasphemy.

What think ye? They answered and said, He is guilty of death.

In the verses above, Caiaphas the Priest ripped his clothes. At face value, it looks as if Caiaphas was so angry that he ripped his clothes, but this is not the case when you understand the laws of Moses pertaining to the conduct and office of the high priest.

Leviticus 10:6

And Moses said unto Aaron, and unto Eleazar and unto Ithamar, his sons, Uncover not your heads, neither rend (rip) your clothes; lest ye die, and lest wrath come upon all the people: but let your brethren, the whole house of Israel, bewail the burning which the LORD hath kindled.

Leviticus 21:10

And he that is the high priest among his brethren, upon whose head the anointing oil was poured, and that is consecrated to put on the garments, shall not uncover his head, nor rend (rip) his clothes;

You can now see the significance of Caiaphas ripping his clothes. Caiaphas the high priest broke the Law, and because he did this, he lost the Levitical priesthood spiritually. The Levitical priesthood was also physically ripped away from Israel in AD70, or 30 years after Christ's death with the fulfilment of Christ's prophecy against the temple in Matthew 24.

Matthew 24:1-2

And Jesus went out, and departed from the temple: and his disciples came to him for to shew him the buildings of the temple.

And Jesus said unto them, See ye not all these things? verily I say unto you, There shall not be left here one stone upon another, that shall not be thrown down.

These events were very significant because they show the restoration of the Melchizedek priesthood under Christ as King and Priest. The priestly tribe of Levi and the kingly tribe of Judah, came to an end at the death of Christ.

It Gets Deeper

When Christ was on the Cross, the Bible reveals that the Roman soldiers divided His clothes amongst themselves, but they cast lots for His coat or mantle. Casting lots is where people use pebbles or straws to make decisions. I guess you could liken it to using rock, paper, scissors, today.

John 19:24

They said therefore among themselves, Let us not rend it, but cast lots for it, whose it shall be: that the scripture might be fulfilled, which saith, They parted my raiment among them, and for my vesture they did cast lots. These things therefore the soldiers did.

You may wonder why I am pointing to this Scripture in regards to the priesthood. Well, if the Romans ripped Jesus' coat, then the Levitical priesthood that was ripped from Chaiphas and given to Him earlier that day, would have also been ripped from Him(Jesus). This is why they unknowingly cast lots for Jesus' coat. After His death, burial and resurrection, both the kingly and the priestly offices were united as one under Him. Interestingly,

Pontius Pilate called Jesus the King of the Jews, and the Roman soldiers respected Jesus' priesthood by not ripping His coat.

So the first people to see Jesus' kingship and priesthood were the unbelieving Gentile Romans, not the Jews. Obviously, they didn't do this knowingly, but I thought it was interesting to point out. The main thing to understand is that we are NOT under Levitical law, but under the Melchizedek Order of Christ. On the Cross, Christ changed the priesthood from Levitical to the Melchizedek one, and in doing so, He changed the Law.

Rev 1:6
And hath made us kings and priests unto God and his Father; to him be glory and dominion for ever and ever. Amen.

Rev 5:10
And hast made us unto our God kings and priests: and we shall reign on the earth.

The death, burial and resurrection of Christ opened and closed so many doors, that the more you study Jesus, the more your mind is blown.

YOUR TRUE
KINGDOM
Identity
THE MAJESTY WITHIN

CHAPTER #5

CHAPTER #5

You Are The Body Of Christ

As Believers, we are not only individuals members of the body of Christ, we are actually THE BODY of Christ, and He is the Head. The whole body is called the body of Christ and we are a part of it. Christian means Christ-like. This is one definition of the word, BUT we are not simply Christ-like, we are Christ. Let me explain. The Bible says;

Romans 8:29

For whom he did foreknow, he also did predestinate to be conformed to the image of his Son, *that he might be the firstborn among many brethren.*

2 Corinthians 3:18

But we all, with open face beholding as in a glass the glory of the Lord, are changed into the same image from glory to glory, even as by the Spirit of the Lord.

We are His Image. Christian means Christ-like, BUT we can't be like His Image because the Bible says that we ARE His Image. Let me take it a little deeper for you. Your arm is a part of your body, your arm is not like a part of your body; your arm IS your body. So, if we are the body of Christ, the arm is not separate from the body of Christ, the arm is the body. Having the label "Christian", is the main contributor to why our identity has been warped by religion, why we don't know who we are and we see ourselves as something different; we see ourselves as lower than what we really are.

If you know that you are the body of Christ, then there are certain things you're not going to be taking from people. If you know that you are a part of a royal family, there are certain mindsets that you are not going to receive from the world. If you know you're an ambassador for Christ, then you know that you are a spokesperson for God and you speak on behalf of His Kingdom. When you speak the things of God, you are in your position and you have all authority to speak on the behalf of Him, why? Well, that's because you're an ambassador and that's what ambassadors do. As Believers and disciples, these are the concepts we need to understand.

You still don't believe that we are Christ? Let me share with you this powerful Scripture;

1 John 4:17
Herein is our love made perfect, that we may have boldness in the day of judgment: because as he is, so are we in this world.

Did you see that? The Apostle John said that *as He is, so are we in this world*! Who is the apostle referring to? He is referring to you as the Believer. As Christ is right now in Heaven, SEATED in the place of Power, so are we here on the earth today. This means that we are His representatives. When people see us, they are supposed to see the Christ that dwells inside of us.

Colossians 1:27
To whom God would make known what is the riches of the glory of this mystery among the Gentiles; which is Christ in you, the hope of glory:

It is a very deep revelation when you begin to unpack it. You must understand that we are partakers of God's divine nature. The only thing that is like God on the earth right now is a Believer.

2 Peter 1:4
Whereby are given unto us exceeding great and precious promises: that by these ye might be partakers of the divine nature, having escaped the corruption that is in the world through lust.

I am not saying that you are literally Jesus Christ who walked throughout Israel 2000 years ago, proclaiming the gospel of the Kingdom, that is not what I am saying, BUT, with the death, burial, resurrection and ascension of Jesus, He ushered in a total new era for those who believe in His name. The Bible says that we are a new creation, that in Christ there are no males or females. Who can this be? Well, that would be us, the born again Believers, because Jesus made us a new creation or a new creature.

2 Corinthians 5:17

Therefore if any man be in Christ, he is a new creature: old things are passed away; behold, all things are become new.

Let me explain this powerful Scripture to you. Adam looked just like God because he was made in His Image (Gen 1:26), but when Adam sinned, he lost the Image of God and his children were made in the image of sinful man and not in the Image of God.

Gen 5:3

And Adam lived an hundred and thirty years, and begat a son in his own likeness, and after his image; and called his name Seth:

All humans have Adam's fallen image and all humans look like Adam. As for the born again Believer, we look like Christ because we have His Image.

Romans 8:29

For whom he did foreknow, he also did predestinate to be conformed to the image of his Son, that he might be the firstborn among many brethren.

The word, conformed, in Greek means, "sharing the same inner essence and identity, showing similar behaviour from having the same essential nature". We bear the Image and form of Christ.

2 Corinthians 3:18

But we all, with open face beholding as in a glass the glory of the Lord, are changed into the same image from glory to glory, even as by the Spirit of the Lord.

There are so many other scriptures which teach that the born again Believer's spirit is not the same as an unbeliever's, as one is dead and the other is alive. The Holy Spirit is what brought these amazing metamorphoses.

Now, this is where it starts to get a little bit deep as we begin to unpack this concept of being part of the body of Christ.

What is the Body of Christ, or The Church?

A lot of people think the Church is a building, but the Church is not a building; it is a body of Believers. The word Church in the Greek, is the word, Ecclesia, or the called out ones. There are some Believers that are very familiar with the meaning of the word, Ecclesia, or the called out ones, BUT that's where their understanding of the word ends. We are about to go deep.

Matthew 16:18

And I say also unto thee, That thou art Peter, and upon this rock I will build my church; and the gates of hell shall not prevail against it.

Jesus uses the word, Church, or like I said earlier, "Ecclesia", although the Greeks had ecclesias or Churches over three hundred years before Jesus walked the shores of Galilee. If you asked an ancient Greek speaker what was an ecclesia, he would tell you that it was a "political assembly of citizens". For many Believers, the Church is a place you attend on a Sunday for fellowship, to hear a sermon, worship and Sunday school for your children.

Now, don't get me wrong, this is all great stuff, but when you begin to understand that that church is actually a place where the citizens of Heaven, aka the Believers, are supposed to gather to discuss and create Kingdom strategies on how to spread our King's influence into the earth, it will shed more light on what Jesus said to Peter in *Matthew 16:18*.

Jesus said to Peter, upon this rock I will build my political assembly of citizens (the Church). (As we are on this subject, Jesus was not saying that He was going to build the Church upon Peter. He was saying that He would build His Church or political assembly of citizens, on Peter's confession that Jesus was the *Christ, the Son of the living God*. This confession is the very foundation that the Church was built on. Without it, there would be no Church.

Jesus said that He will build His Church. This would mean that there were other churches around at the time of Christ, like the Sanhedrin Council. The Sanhedrin Council was made up of Jewish aristocrats, the heads of rich and powerful families like Joseph of Arimathea, and religious leaders like Nicodemus. The head of this council was the High Priest and at the time of Jesus, that would have been Caiaphas. Everyone in the Sanhedrin Council were called-out Citizens that discussed political matters, and Jesus was always a hot topic for the Sanhedrin Council.

This is where it begins to get very powerful because a Church is a government, and governments are made up of Citizens who are given the authority to rule. This is what Governments do. For example, in a democracy, the people vote in Citizens from their country to represent them within their country's government. All governments rule, whether it's a communist, dictatorship, aristocracy, Colonialist or Socialist. Those who are a part of that government, rule over the people and resources. The Church is God's government on Earth, and we are supposed to be bringing people under the rulership and Lordship of Christ, who is the head of our Government.

The Church is the government of God on the earth, so in essence, every Believer is a governmental official on official business on the earth. Our job and mission is the same as Jesus', as He stated in;

Luke 4:18-19

The Spirit of the Lord is upon me, because he hath anointed me to preach the gospel to the poor; he hath sent me to heal the brokenhearted, to preach deliverance to the captives, and recovering of sight to the blind, to set at liberty them that are bruised,

To preach the acceptable year of the Lord.

This is what the Government or the Church is supposed to be obsessed with, because this is what Jesus was obsessed with, and we are His body and He is the head. God's plan for the people of the earth has not changed.

2 Peter 3:9

The Lord is not slack concerning his promise, as some men count slackness; but is longsuffering to us-ward, not willing that any should perish, but that all should come to repentance.

The Will Of God

The Will of God is a mystery for many Believers today, because it has never really been properly explained. Understanding the Will of God seems to only have been granted to our Apostles, Prophets and the spiritually deep saints that walk amongst us. Understanding the Will of God is not really that deep at all, and to tell you the truth, it's VERY basic.

As I was pondering the Will of God the other day, God showed me a man writing out his will. He was writing down what he wanted to happen to his possession after he died.

You see, the word "will" means desires and wishes, it's as simple as that. When someone is writing a will before they die, they are giving out instructions of what should take place with their property and personal belongings after their passing. So, the Will of God is the same sort of thing. It is all about God's wishes and desires. Therefore, as Believers, we Must understand what God's wishes and desires are, generally and personally. What does God want for the whole of mankind? What does God want for you on a day-to-day basis?

God's desire originally was to expand His Kingdom by creating Heaven and Earth and filling it with His sons. It was God's will in creating the Earth and to give it to mankind to rule over. But as you know, Adam lost the Earth realm by rebelling against God.

But the Apostle Peter teaches us that God is not willing, or it's not God's desire or wish for anyone to perish, but for all of us to come to repentance.

This is why in Genesis 3:15, He promised a Saviour that would destroy the works of the devil and reconcile mankind back to God. Out of God's desires and wishes, His plan for man's "sin" situation was birthed.

Genesis 3:15 - **The promised Saviour**

And I will put enmity (war) between thee (Satan) and the woman, and between thy seed and her seed (Jesus); it shall bruise thy head, and thou shalt bruise his heel.

1 John 3:8 - **Satan's head or authority crushed**

He that committeth sin is of the devil; for the devil sinneth from the beginning. For this purpose the Son of God (Jesus) was manifested, that he might destroy the works of the devil.

2 Cor 5:19 - **Through Christ, the world can come back to God**

To wit, that God was in Christ, reconciling (bringing back) the world unto himself, not imputing their trespasses unto them; and hath committed unto us the word of reconciliation.

Remember, Peter said that God is not willing that any should perish but all should come to repentance.

Before the flood of Noah, God was going to destroy all of the humans on the Earth because they had become corrupted and evil to the core. But God's ultimate desire is not to kill or destroy humans, but for them all to come to repentance. God used Noah to create a way of escape because His desires and wishes are for mankind to live and prosper, and not to be destroyed in the lake of fire.

Ezekiel 33:11

Say unto them, As I live, saith the Lord GOD, I have no pleasure in the death of the wicked; but that the wicked turn from his way and live: turn ye, turn ye from your evil ways; for why will ye die, O house of Israel?

Not only did God commission Noah to build an Ark, He also sent him to preach to all the wicked people that were alive at that time.

2 Peter 2:5

And spared not the old world, but saved Noah the eighth person, a preacher of righteousness, bringing in the flood upon the world of the ungodly;

So, as the body of Christ or God's physical government on the earth, it is our job to understand what are God's wishes and desires for our communities, friends, family, finances, and health. What is God wishes and desires for world leaders and the heads of industries? What are God's wishes and desires for you and your life? As the body of Christ, we have to ask ourselves these questions.

YOUR TRUE KINGDOM IDENTITY

YOUR TRUE KINGDOM

Identity

THE MAJESTY WITHIN

CHAPTER #6

CHAPTER #6

The Bride Of Christ

We are Christ's wife or we are betrothed to Christ. Unlike an engagement which sets an intention to marry, a betrothal ceremony requires the couple to commit to marry. When a Hebrew male betrothed a woman, he would leave her with her father for one year, and go and build a house and then officially marry her. The house the man builds was sometimes an extension on his father's house. This is why Jesus says in;

John 14:2-3
In my Father's house are many mansions: if it were not so, I would have told you. I go to prepare a place for you.

And if I go and prepare a place for you, I will come again, and receive you unto myself; that where I am, there ye may be also.

These verses are about a Hebrew wedding where Jesus receives His wife.

Jesus loves us and we are going to be married to Him. As a man, you love your wife-to-be whom you're going to be married to, and you will not abuse or mistreat her. Jesus loves His bride and He lavishes her with whatever she needs. There is a certain confidence a bride has when she has been betrothed because she knows that her future is secure. She knows that her husband is coming to collect her and take her to a house with land.

When we understand just the basics of Hebrew culture, it will take our biblical understanding to a higher level, because most of the Bible is written in Hebrew, and it's about the Hebrews. Well, that was until Jesus died and there was a major shift, but that topic is for a different book.

When Jesus teaches about the parable of the ten virgins, five foolish and five wise, the groom left and then came back. If you understand about Jewish weddings, you will know that when the groom has finished building his house, he turns up unannounced to collect his bride. Remember, when Jesus was in His ministry, He was talking to the Hebrew people and not to Gentiles. So, sometimes what Jesus' teachings mean to us and what they mean to the Hebrew people, could be very different. When you hear the name Christian, the things I've just said are not the first things that pop into your head.

When someone says you're a christian, they are not thinking that you're a king, an ambassador, a son of God, a citizen of the kingdom, a priest, the bride of Christ, the body of Christ, or a disciple of Christ. They're not really thinking that at all, they just think you go church on a Sunday and you read the Bible. When we understand the riches of our Kingdom Identity, things like prophecy, the word of wisdom, the word of knowledge, miracles, faith and other giftings, come easier.

You have authority, but how do you understand your authority? Well, if you don't understand what a king is, then how can you understand your authority? This is why so many scriptures do not work for us, or the Bible does not seem to be producing for us what is written within its pages. This is because we don't know who we are. If I say that you are a king, then there are certain things you will not accept into your life. As a king, there are certain types of lifestyles you will not pursue because you're a king. Kings don't go to the crack house, Kings don't sleep around, Kings are regal. Kings have authority, so when things are going out of alignment and things are not going right, a king has authority to speak, and it gets done.

Ecclesiastes 8:4
Where the word of a king is, there is power: and who may say unto him, What doest thou?

When demons are messing up your life, you have to use your authority as a king and tell them to leave. You have to take authority over low self-esteem, evil thoughts and fear in the name of Jesus. All of the powers of the demonic are under your feet because you're a king. If you think you're just a humble Christian who goes to church on a Sunday, and you pray and read the Bible, how are you going to understand your authority? For you to understand your authority in Christ, you have to see it from a king's perspective.

We are the bride of Christ because Jesus had to remarry us as a consequence of Adam's adultery.

The Garden OF Eden From A Different Perspective

The Garden of Eden and the creation of man goes a lot deeper than what we have been taught in church. Genesis 1:26 reveals to us that man was made in the Image of God. Further to this, 1 John 1:5 teaches that God is light, and in Him is no darkness at all. So, that means that Adam was made from light and had some sort of light covering. This is how Adam and Eve knew that they were naked when they ate from the tree of the knowledge of good and evil.

Genesis 2:16-17

And the Lord God commanded the man, saying, Of every tree of the garden thou mayest freely eat:

But of the tree of the knowledge of good and evil, thou shalt not eat of it: for in the day that thou eatest thereof thou shalt surely die.

This command was a covenant that God made with Adam. As long as Adam kept it, he would remain in fellowship with God. Now, as we all know, Adam and Eve ate from the tree, and perfect fellowship was broken between them and God. Now, this is where it gets very interesting, because in;

Genesis 3:23-24

Therefore the Lord God sent him forth from the garden of Eden, to till the ground from whence he was taken.

So he drove out the man; and he placed at the east of the garden of Eden Cherubims, and a flaming sword which turned every way, to keep the way of the tree of life.

In verse 23, God sends man out of the Garden of Eden, and that word *sent* in the Hebrew, means to send away, to let loose, to dismiss and divorce. In verse 24, it states that God drove out the Man; well, that word *drove* in the Hebrew means to divorce and to put away. So in essence, God divorced the man for committing adultery, and we know that adultery is covenant breaking or being unfaithful. How did Adam break his covenant with God? Well, he came in covenant with someone else i.e., Satan. He was unfaithful. Now, am I saying that Adam and Eve had intercorse with the serpent? No, I am not, and no, I don't believe in the serpent seed doctrine. All I'm saying is that God divorced the man for breaking the covenant.

In God divorcing Adam, He also divorced the whole of mankind. You will see God come into covenant with Israel, but they were unfaithful to Him through their disobedience and idolatry. Throughout the Old Testament, Israel was continuously called a harlot, unfaithful and an adulterous nation by many of the Prophets. God's original plan has always been to be married to mankind. This is where Jesus comes into God's equation. You see, Jesus is God manifested in the flesh, and because of the death of Christ, the Believers became God's bride.

The Creation Of Eve

Genesis 2:21-23

And the LORD God caused a deep sleep to fall upon Adam, and he slept: and he took one of his ribs, and closed up the flesh instead thereof;

And the rib, which the LORD God had taken from man, made he a woman, and brought her unto the man.

And Adam said, This is now bone of my bones, and flesh of my flesh: she shall be called Woman, because she was taken out of Man.

When God created Adam, Eve was already present inside of him; all God did was to pull her out. Eve came from Adam's rib and the word *rib*, means *side* in Hebrew. Eve was made from the very substance that Adam was created from. She has a spirit, a soul and a body just like Adam. In God's eyes, Adam and Eve were one entity, not two, as Eve was just a different side of Adam. We can see that God saw them as one entity, because the Bible teaches that God cast Adam out of the Garden, not Eve, but we know He cast them both out. Also, in Genesis chapter 5, it states:

Gen 5:2
Male and female created he them; and blessed them, and called their name Adam, in the day when they were created.

You see, God called THEIR name, Adam. Now, let's get back to Jesus on the Cross. Where was Jesus pierced and what came out?

John 19:34
But one of the soldiers with a spear pierced his side, and forthwith came there out blood and water.

A Roman soldier pierced Jesus' side! The word *side* in the Greek, is *"pleura"* which means *"rib"*. In Genesis, God took a rib from Adam and the Hebrew word for rib is *"ṣēlā`-"* which means *"side"*. So, the same place Adam's wife (Eve) was taken from, is the same place Jesus' wife (the Church) was taken from.

The Blood and water that came from Jesus' side represents the Church. The Blood is the New Testament and washing away of our sins, and the water represents the new birth. When we accept Jesus, He becomes our husband and we become His bride and ultimately, His wife. Jesus is the last Adam, and the last Adam, just like the first, has a wife. Because the first Adam Sinned, he condemned his wife and the whole of the human race to death. Remember, Adam and Eve's eyes were opened only after Adam ate from the tree, not when Eve ate from it. God gave the command not to eat from the tree of the knowledge of good and evil directly to Adam, not to Eve. So after he ate from the tree, the whole of mankind fell.

Genesis 3:6-7a

And when the woman saw that the tree was good for food, and that it was pleasant to the eyes, and a tree to be desired to make one wise, she took of the fruit thereof, and did eat, and gave also unto her husband with her; and he did eat.

And the eyes of them both were opened,

Romans 5:12

Wherefore, as by one man sin entered into the world, and death by sin; and so death passed upon all men, for that all have sinned.

Now, this is the exciting part. You see, Jesus can never sin and He is perfect, and we are His bride, therefore, we cannot sin because His Church is perfect. Yes, I am fully aware of what the Apostle John said;

1 John 1:8
If we say we have no sin, we deceive ourselves, and the truth is not in us.

We just need to Identify where the sin is, and it is not in our spirit, the part of us where the Spirit of God resides. The sin is in the fleshy part of our being. Remember, we are a trichotomy i.e., we are spirit, soul and body. Your flesh is corrupted and so is your soul, BUT your spirit is blood brought and perfect. If it was not, then you could not be inside of Christ. Let me show you. Jesus and God ultimately are the same person, whether you believe in the trinity or the oneness of God, and we are in Christ. The Bible teaches that there is no darkness inside of God, 1 John 1:5. Sin is darkness and error, so for us to be in Christ, that would mean that we must be light because darkness cannot dwell inside of God. This shows us that it's our flesh and soul which are dark, and our spirit is perfect in heavenly places in Christ Jesus.

This book is all about your true identity in Christ. The New Birth is a spiritual transformation and not a physical one. We need to start seeing ourselves as Jesus' spiritually perfect bride, and when we do, our lives will never be the same.

YOUR TRUE KINGDOM

Identity

THE MAJESTY WITHIN

CHAPTER #7

CHAPTER #7

Your Kingdom Citizenship

The first thing we have to establish is what a Citizen is and what it means to be a citizen of a country.

- A Citizen is someone who is born in a country = this is a way that a person acquires citizenship.

- A Citizen is someone who lives in a country = You can live in a country and still not be a Citizen of that country.

- The Word Citizen means "belonging". So, A Citizen is someone who belongs to a country and is entitled to the rights, privileges and freedoms of that country.

We all know that in the beginning, God created Heaven and Earth, and that Heaven is God's throne and the earth is His footstool. The Kingdom of Heaven and the kingdom of the earth were both connected before the fall of man.

When the angels were created, they were automatically Citizens of the Kingdom of Heaven; this was the same thing that happened to Adam when he was created. Adam was given authority to rule over the kingdom of the earth, and because the earth was an extension or colony of the Kingdom of Heaven, Adam was automatically a Kingdom citizen. Adam's wife was also a Kingdom citizen automatically. Every human that would have been born, if Adam did not disobey God, would have also gained automatic Kingdom citizenship.

Citizenship Lost

One of the saddest parts of the Bible is when Adam and Eve were expelled from the Garden of Eden because they rebelled against the sovereign King of Heaven. When Adam and Eve were expelled out of the Garden of Eden, they automatically lost their citizenship and their access to Kingdom things. As a side note, Satan, the serpent or Lucifer also lost his Kingdom citizenship because of his rebellion against the King of Heaven. With the loss of Kingdom Citizenship also came the loss of the privileges and rights associated with being a Kingdom Citizen. Access to Eden was revoked, access to eternal life was revoked, Adam's right to rule over all the resources of the earth was revoked. These are just a few things which Adam and Eve lost.

Citizenship Restored

When it comes to the Cross, we think that Jesus only died for our sins so that we can go to Heaven when we die. That is somewhat true, but the death, burial and resurrection of Jesus has so many different dimensions to it, that it is mind blowing when you dig deeper. With the death of Jesus on the Cross, Kingdom citizenship is now offered to all mankind for free!

For most Believers, the revelation of Citizenship has never been explained to them, or they just don't know anything about it. The Kingdom message that Jesus preached during His time here on the earth is powerful. When we begin to understand that the Bible is not a religious book and that the message of the Bible is not about religion, topics about Citizenship become very exciting. When it dawns upon you that you are a citizen of a different country, i.e., Heaven, your life will change forever. Kingdom Citizenship is mentioned in the New Testament by Jesus, Paul and the writer of the Book of Hebrews.

Acts 16:12 describes Philippi as a Roman colony as well as a chief city. Many retired Roman soldiers took up residence in Philippi, so this could be one of the reasons why Paul mentioned Kingdom Citizenship in his letter to the Philippian Church, because they would have understood that term very well, as they were also citizens of a far country, i.e., Rome.

Philippians 1:27

Only let your conversation (Citizenship) *be as it becometh the gospel of Christ: that whether I come and see you, or else be absent, I may hear of your affairs, that ye stand fast in one spirit, with one mind striving together for the faith of the gospel;*

Philippians 3:20

For our conversation (Citizenship) *is in heaven; from whence also we look for the Saviour, the Lord Jesus Christ:*

Heaven's Register

When Jesus sent out His twelve to preach the gospel of the Kingdom to the villages and towns, they were happy that the demons were subjected to them by the name of Jesus. But Jesus explains to His disciples that they should rejoice because they have Kingdom Citizenship and not because they casted demons out.

Luke 10:20

Notwithstanding in this rejoice not, that the spirits are subject unto you; but rather rejoice, because your names are written in heaven.

We are Kingdom Citizens and our names are written on Heaven's register. Our names are logged in the main database of Heaven.

Hebrews 12:22-23

But ye are come unto mount Sion, and unto the city of the living God, the heavenly Jerusalem, and to an innumerable company of angels,

To the general assembly and church of the firstborn, which are written (Registered) in heaven, and to God the Judge of all, and to the spirits of just men made perfect,

Revelation 21:27

And there shall in no wise enter into it any thing that defileth, neither whatsoever worketh abomination, or maketh a lie: but they which are written in the Lamb's book of life.

This is the same register or book that is opened at the Great White Throne Judgment. The Lamb's book of life contains all of the names of the citizens of the Kingdom of Heaven. Only Citizens are on a register, and only registered citizens can gain access to Heaven or the new Heaven and new Earth in the future.

Did You Know That You Are An Alien?

Many years ago, a pop artist called Sting, released a song called "Englishman In New York". In this song, he says, "I'm a legal alien, I'm an Englishman in New York". A legal alien is someone who is in a country in which they do not belong . If you are in a place where you do not belong, you are called an "Alien". How does this relate to us as Believers? Well, because we are residing here on the earth, we are called aliens. Get Hollywood and films out of your mind. But having said that, in the movies, you can tell who is the alien and who is not because the alien looks and acts differently to the non-alien.

The word 'alien' is opposite to the word Citizen, in other words, alien means someone "not belonging". This applies to someone who is in a country and has the right to reside there and operate, but he or she does not belong there.

We are citizens of the Kingdom of Heaven and we are aliens here on the earth. Jesus said, "we are in the world but not of it". Jesus consistently proclaimed that He was not from the earth and that He was from another place or country, i.e., Heaven.

John 8:23
And he said unto them, Ye are from beneath; I am from above: ye are of this world; I am not of this world.

John 17:16
They (The Believers) *are not of the world, even as I* (Jesus) *am not of the world.*

We receive our Kingdom Of Heaven citizenship when we are born again.

John 3:3-5

Jesus answered and said unto him, Verily, verily, I say unto thee, Except a man be born again, he cannot see the kingdom of God.

Nicodemus saith unto him, How can a man be born when he is old? can he enter the second time into his mother's womb, and be born?

Jesus answered, Verily, verily, I say unto thee, Except a man be born of water and of the Spirit, he cannot enter into the kingdom of God.

One of the things which all born again Believers must recognise is that on the outside, we look just like everyone else, but on the inside there has been a change. Before we became born again, our spirit was dead towards God, but now we are born again, the Holy Spirit has quickened us and we are alive to God. The Bible teaches that we are a totally New Creation where, before, we inherited our dead spirit from Adam, and now we have inherited a quickening spirit from the Lord.

Some Believers operate with dual citizenship. These are carnal and lukewarm Christians and it's impossible to operate that way. You are either in God's Kingdom or you are not!

Rev 3:16

So then because thou art lukewarm, and neither cold nor hot, I will spue thee out of my mouth.

Kingdoms Take Care Of Their Citizens

If you were in a foreign land and for some reason you were arrested and you had no money or help, it would be up to your country to look after you by sending a lawyer to intercede and fight on your behalf. We see this on the news all the time, for example, when a student takes pictures in North Korea or joins some mass protest in Beijing and gets arrested, their country's embassy has to get involved. One of the main responsibilities of a kingdom is to take care of its citizens, whether at home or abroad.

Citizens And Subjects

I will first start off by saying that we are Citizens of a Kingdom and not Subjects. The biggest difference between Citizens and Subjects is that Citizens have rights and Subjects do not. To be a subject means that you are under the dominion or control of someone. Captured nations of old would be subjugated to the ruler or king of the dominant kingdom. Israel were subjects in Babylon, they were not Babylonian citizens. Just like in the Book of Esther, it was so simple for Haman to get King Ahasuerus to sign into law the destruction of the Jews. Do you think Haman could get the king to pass that evil law against the

Citizens of Persia? No way, why? Because Citizens have been granted rights and protection from the king.

We could take this a little bit further so that you can get a fuller understanding of how powerful citizenship really is. In the Book of Acts 16:11-40, it tells us how Paul was in Philippi, which was a Roman colony in Macedonia. Paul and Silas were beaten for casting a devil out of a young girl and for preaching the gospel and then they were cast into jail.

The following day, the magistrates ordered the prison guards to let Paul and Silas out of the prison. The magistrates then found out that they were Roman Citizens and they feared greatly. Why were the magistrates fearful? Well, that is because they thought that Paul and Silas were Jewish subjects with no rights. You cannot treat citizens the same as you treat subjects because Citizens have rights. The magistrate knew they were in big trouble if Paul and Silas chose to take the matter to the Roman governor of that region.

Citizen Rights And Privileges

I am physically a citizen of the United Kingdom, and as such, I have access to certain rights and privileges. Let me name a few: I have the right to hold a British passport, full civic rights – this includes the right to vote in elections and the right to stand for public office; Free

NHS medical care and I have no restrictions on my right to work. I have the right to live in the UK.

What we need to understand is that spiritually, all born again Believers are Citizens of the Kingdom Of Heaven, and we also have rights and privileges as Spiritual Beings. We have the right to access all that the Kingdom has to offer us, or as I like to put it, we have total access to the commonwealth of the Kingdom.

The commonwealth of the Kingdom of Heaven means that all of the riches, honour and glory is common amongst all of the born again Believers.

The Beatitudes in Matthew chapter 5:3-12, Gives us a taste of some of our Kingdom privileges:

3   *Blessed are the poor in spirit: for theirs is the kingdom of heaven.*

4   *Blessed are they that mourn: for they shall be comforted.*

5   *Blessed are the meek: for they shall inherit the earth.*

6   *Blessed are they which do hunger and thirst after righteousness: for they shall be filled.*

7   *Blessed are the merciful: for they shall obtain mercy.*

8 *Blessed are the pure in heart: for they shall see God.*

9 *Blessed are the peacemakers: for they shall be called the children of God.*

10 *Blessed are they which are persecuted for righteousness' sake: for theirs is the kingdom of heaven.*

11 *Blessed are ye, when men shall revile you, and persecute you, and shall say all manner of evil against you falsely, for my sake.*

12 *Rejoice, and be exceeding glad: for great is your reward in heaven: for so persecuted they the prophets which were before you.*

The Apostle Peter and Paul reveal to us a few more:

1 Timothy 6:17

Charge them that are rich in this world, that they be not highminded, nor trust in uncertain riches, but in the living God, who giveth us richly all things to enjoy;

Ephesians 1:3

Blessed be the God and Father of our Lord Jesus Christ, who hath blessed us with all spiritual blessings in heavenly places in Christ:

Romans 8:17

And if children, then heirs; heirs of God, and joint-heirs with Christ; if so be that we suffer with him, that we may be also glorified together.

2 Peter 1:3

According as his divine power hath given unto us all things that pertain unto life and godliness, through the knowledge of him that hath called us to glory and virtue:

The above are just a few Scriptures which reveal to us the privileges of being a Kingdom Citizen.

All Kingdom Citizens are given Kingdom rights and there are many of them. If we fully understand our Kingdom rights, then it will not be so easy for the devil to deceive us. I will share a few scriptures to give you a small taste of our Kingdom Rights.

We have the Right to freedom or not to be bound by Satan.

Galatians 5:1

Stand fast therefore in the liberty wherewith Christ hath made us free, and be not entangled again with the yoke of bondage.

We have the Right to Healing.

Isaiah 53:5

But he was wounded for our transgressions, he was bruised for our iniquities: the chastisement of our peace was upon him; and with his stripes we are healed.

It's our Right to be able to have an audience with the King to receive mercy and grace.

Hebrews 4:16

Let us therefore come boldly unto the throne of grace, that we may obtain mercy, and find grace to help in time of need.

We have a Right to become and to be the sons of God, which also has a claim to be part of God's Royal Family.

John 1:12

But as many as received him, to them gave he power to become the sons of God, even to them that believe on his name:

We have a Right to be filled with the Holy Spirit.

Acts 2:38

Then Peter said unto them, Repent, and be baptized every one of you in the name of Jesus Christ for the remission of sins, and ye shall receive the gift of the Holy Ghost.

We have a right to share in the commonwealth of the Kingdom of Heaven.

Philippians 4:19

But my God shall supply all your need according to his riches in glory by Christ Jesus.

YOUR TRUE KINGDOM

Identity

THE MAJESTY WITHIN

CHAPTER #8

CHAPTER #8

Your Discipleship

What Is A Disciple?

This is the first thing we must establish before we continue with the identity of our discipleship. Disciple is the word "mathētés" in the Greek, which means a learner or a pupil: to take it a little deeper, it generally means "one who engages in learning through instruction from another; a pupil or an apprentice". As Believers, we automatically think that a disciple is only one of the twelve who followed Christ, but this is not so. This also goes for the word, Church, we automatically think it means the "body of Christ or a building", but the word church is not a word exclusive to Christians as I've explained in an earlier chapter.

Have you ever heard of the ancient Greek philosopher, Socrates? Well, Socrates was alive 400 years before

Christ. He had a disciple whose name was Plato, and Plato had a disciple called Aristotle. Before Christ, many thought leaders had disciples, even religious leaders had disciples that sat at their feet. Interestingly, Mary sat at Jesus' feet showing that she was one of His disciples, (not one of the twelve) but one of His followers who learned from Him.

Luke 10:39

And she had a sister called Mary, which also sat at Jesus' feet, and heard his word.

In the New Testament, John the Baptist had disciples that followed him. The Gospel of John reveals to us that Andrew, the brother of Simon Peter, was one of them.

John 1:40

One of the two which heard John speak, and followed him, was Andrew, Simon Peter's brother.

There were many Jews that heard the ministry of John the Baptist about a coming Messiah like Apollos, who became one of his disciples, or who sat at his feet. We also see the Apostle Paul's encounter with twelve followers of John the Baptist in Acts chapter 19. In this chapter, you can see that John the Baptist had a main group of twelve disciples and one lone disciple, Apollos in Acts 18:24-25. That makes 13. There is a similarity of this with Jesus' disciples. The main group of twelve apostles in Acts 1 and one lone Apostle Paul in Acts 9, adds up to 13 Disciples of Christ. The Bible is filled with these interesting details.

The Privileges Of Being A Disciple

When you are a disciple of Jesus, you have access to hidden wisdom, knowledge, secrets and mysteries that have been hidden from the foundations of the world. The whole of the New Testament was written by the disciples of Christ (not just some of the twelve). In the four Gospels, all of the revelation shared was by Christ Himself, but as we read from Acts to Revelation, every revelation shared is by His disciples through the Holy Spirit.

Matthew 13:10 -11

And the disciples came, and said unto him, Why speakest thou unto them in parables?

He answered and said unto them, Because it is given unto you to know the mysteries of the kingdom of heaven, but to them it is not given.

Just imagine being able to ask Jesus the meaning of His teachings and Him personally answering you in a one on one session? This is the privileged position that disciples have. Many times throughout the Gospels, the disciples asked Jesus questions like, "why was this man born blind?" or "why did the scribes say that Elijah must first come?" Or the questions they asked Him about adultery.

The disciples were very privileged to see the Master at work everyday for over three years. They beheld all of the miracles, the healings, the teachings, the prophecies, the signs and wonders that were all carried out before their very eyes. Us as modern day believers, are also in the same privileged positions as the disciples of Jesus, as we all have seen the powerful work of the Holy Spirit through the hands of the Church.

The Purpose Of A Disciple

The purpose of every disciple was to pattern or become a replica of their teacher. So, when you see and hear the disciples, they sound just like their teacher. They have the same philosophies, beliefs and they head in the same direction as the teacher they follow.

Matthew 10:24-25

The disciple is not above his master, nor the servant above his lord.

It is enough for the disciple that he be as his master, and the servant as his lord. If they have called the master of the house Beelzebub, how much more shall they call them of his household?

Jesus said that as disciples, we cannot be greater than Him, but we can become like Him.

When Jesus started His ministry, He understood that He could not do it alone because as a man, He would need help. If Jesus could complete His ministry without help, He would have, but because He was a man, He was limited (obviously as God He was unlimited, that's a conversation that is outside the scope of this book). Jesus lived by example, and as a man, He had the Holy Ghost inside of Him the same way you are a human with the Holy Spirit inside of you. So, even though Jesus and us humans have the unlimited power residing inside of us, we still need help because we can only do so much before we begin to burn out.

Just imagine Jesus trying to organise a gathering of 5000 and 4000 people, or visiting over 200 different villages, towns and cities throughout Israel to preach the Gospel of the Kingdom on foot by Himself. Imagine Jesus rowing across the Sea of Galilee multiple times by Himself. If Jesus had no disciples, He would have been stampeded and crushed by crowds many times. Could He have done it all by Himself? Maybe! Without disciples, the message of the Kingdom would have properly ended when He ascended into Heaven, as there would have been no one to carry on His ministry on the earth.

So, now you can understand why the first thing Jesus did after humiliating the Devil in the wilderness, was to choose 12 key disciples. Just imagine the privilege to be chosen by the only begotten Son of God.

The Power Of Being A Disciple

Being a disciple of the Master is such a powerful thing. An amazing thing happened in Luke 9:1 when Jesus gave the disciples the ability and authority to move in signs, wonders and miracles. He gave them this power so that they could go and preach the gospel of the Kingdom to the cities and towns that would have been impossible for Jesus to visit.

Luke 9:1

Then he called his twelve disciples together, and gave them power and authority over all devils, and to cure diseases.

After this, He sent another 70 disciples to every city that He would be visiting in the future.

Luke 10:1

After these things the Lord appointed other seventy also, and sent them two and two before his face into every city and place, whither he himself would come.

The authority that Jesus bestowed on His disciples seemed to have been temporary, because in Luke 9:1 they were given the power to cast out evil spirits, and in Luke 9:40 they could not.

The power of the Holy Spirit or the Spirit of God always came upon the Prophets, Priests, Kings and others who were used by God in the Old Testament, temporarily. This temporal empowerment is the same thing that happened to the disciples. This was never God's original plan. God's plan has always been for His Spirit to dwell permanently inside and on man, just like it did with Adam. Adam was made in the Image of God, and the Image of God is His Spirit. But as we all know, Adam lost the Image of God's Spirit when he disobeyed Him in the Garden of Eden.

Genesis 2:7-8

And the Lord God formed man of the dust of the ground, and breathed into his nostrils the breath of life; and man became a living soul.

And the Lord God planted a garden eastward in Eden; and there he put the man whom he had formed.

What is God's breath? God's breath is His Spirit and His Spirit brings life. The breath of life was breathed into man then he came alive. Now God did not breathe oxygen into Adam because a spirit does not need oxygen. Interestingly, Jesus said that He IS life, John 14:6.

God breathed Himself into man. Only then did Adam get access to the Garden of Eden and all of its resources.

Restoring The Image

Jesus said that if He does not leave, then the Image of God that Adam lost could not be restored to those who want it.

John 16:7
Nevertheless I tell you the truth; It is expedient for you that I go away: for if I go not away, the Comforter will not come unto you; but if I depart, I will send him unto you.

The Comforter, which we know is the Holy Ghost, has restored to us the Image of God/Jesus which Adam lost. So, now the same power that Jesus had to do all of the powerful things He did during His ministry, has been given to us the believers, permanently. This happened in the Book of Acts chapter 2 on the day of Pentecost. The disciples of Christ (us) have been empowered to move in ministry and our ministry is to allow God to move through us to bring Kingdom influence to the earth.

How To Become A Powerful Disciple.

Becoming a powerful disciple is all about alignment and keeping our eyes on the Master.

Matthew 6:22
The light of the body is the eye: if therefore thine eye be single, thy whole body shall be full of light.

There are multiple ways to look at this Scripture, but I want to look at it in terms of being full of the teachings of Christ. The more we understand Jesus, the more we understand the Bible and in us understanding the Bible more deeply, the more powerful we will become. You cannot live the abundant life that Jesus spoke about in John 10:10 without having a deep understanding of who Jesus is. So, as disciples, our main goal is to understand Jesus on the deepest level possible.

The Bible teaches that everything we need is in Christ: from wisdom to freedom, power, knowledge, authority, even our day to day physical needs are in Christ.

Matthew 6:33

But seek ye first the kingdom of God, and his righteousness; and all these things shall be added unto you.

This is another scripture that can be looked at from different perspectives and it will give us some powerful insights. Jesus is the King of the Kingdom and He is the righteousness of God. So, if we seek after Jesus, we are seeking after the Kingdom in one aspect. Obviously, this verse goes much deeper than what I have just shared, but those revelations will take me from the point I am sharing about becoming a powerful disciple.

Understanding the two scriptures down below are a must because they are the key to becoming a powerful disciple.

2 Timothy 2:15

Study to shew thyself approved unto God, a workman that needeth not to be ashamed, rightly dividing the word of truth.

Romans 12:2

And be not conformed to this world: but be ye transformed by the renewing of your mind, that ye may prove what is that good, and acceptable, and perfect, will of God.

As disciples, we have to study the Word purposefully and in us studying the Word, it will renew our minds. If you are not learning the things and the ways of Christ by reading the Word, then how can you call yourself a disciple? To increase our power in the Spirit, we have to increase our knowledge of Christ, because He is the key that unlocks EVERYTHING good.

YOUR TRUE KINGDOM

Identity

THE MAJESTY WITHIN

CHAPTER #9

CHAPTER #9

How To Practically Start Walking In Your Kingdom Identity

If you want to start walking in your new identity, you have to understand what I like to call "Kingdom language theory", or you become what you immerse yourself in. Did you know that Jesus came to the earth to give us access to a Kingdom Worldview?

One of my most favourite films of all time is called, "Arrival". Basically, aliens come to Earth and the people of Earth cannot understand the aliens' language. A linguistic expert is sent to decipher the aliens' language and learn how to communicate with them.

This goes on for months, then one of the physicists, who is also a part of the team sent to decipher the alien language, asks the linguistic expert if she has started to perceive the world the same way as the aliens, because she has been studying them for so many months. He called it the "Sapir–Whorf hypothesis" (we will get back to that in a minute).

The linguist professional didn't tell the physicist that she could see the future, as the aliens' language she has been studying allows the person who understands it to perceive time the same way as the aliens do, which is NON-LINEAR.

This takes us to; Language relativity.

The hypothesis of linguistic relativity, also known as the Sapir–Whorf hypothesis, is a principle suggesting that the structure of a language affects its speakers' worldview or cognition, and thus, people's perceptions are relative to their spoken language.

The language you use changes the way you see the world and how you think. Now, let's read a few powerful verses from a perspective that you may not have seen before.

Romans 12:2

And be not conformed to this world: but be ye transformed by the renewing of your mind, that ye may prove what is that good, and acceptable, and perfect, will of God.

There are two words which I want to focus on in this verse, and they are the words "conform" and "transformed". The word "conform" means moulded or shaped, and the word "transformed" means to be changed. So, in essence, Romans 12:2 says;

"Don't be moulded, shaped or behave like the world, but let your moral character be changed by the truth that is inside of you, and when you do, you will understand God's perfect will for your life."

Eph 4:22-24

That ye put off concerning the former conversation the old man, which is corrupt according to the deceitful lusts;

And be renewed in the spirit of your mind;

And that ye put on the new man, which after God is created in righteousness and true holiness.

Again, this verse echoes the same things we read in Romans 12:2. The word "conversation" in this verse does not mean "talking with someone", it actually means conduct, behaviour or lifestyle. So, we must stop acting like the old man and be renewed in the spirit of our mind. If you want to walk in your new Kingdom identity, you have to take off the old man and put on the new by having a renewed mind.

Colossians 3:10

And have put on the new man, which is renewed in knowledge after the image of him that created him:

Again, this verse follows the same principle concerning the new man and how to put it on. The word "renewed" means to be changed or to be transformed by possessing the knowledge of who Christ is. This can only take place if we increase our hunger to understand all the things we can possibly know about God, by allowing His Word to change us.

Colossians 3:2

Set your affection on things above, not on things on the earth.

Here is another key on how to be changed and transformed, and that is by focusing or making spiritual things a priority in your life. This verse is a rewording of Matthew 6:33, where it teaches that we MUST seek the Kingdom first and His righteousness, or simply, "put God first".

Paul had DEEP spiritual revelations and spiritual understanding, and now you know why; it was because of linguistic relativity, or you become what you immerse yourself in. In these verses, Paul teaches us that we need to change the way we speak and think, or we will never be able to put on the New man. We have to have a Kingdom worldview and the only way to do this is to be consumed by the Kingdom of God. Paul had the worldview of a Pharisee and that worldview was very strict and religious. When he gave his life to Jesus and received the Holy Spirit, his language and worldview changed drastically. Paul gives us a snapshot of his religious lifestyle and how he used to think before and after his damascus road experience.

Before Conversion

Galatians 1:13-14

For ye have heard of my conversation (lifestyle, conduct, behaviour) *in time past in the Jews' religion, how that beyond measure I persecuted the church of God, and wasted it:*

And profited in the Jews' religion above many my equals in mine own nation, being more exceedingly zealous of the traditions of my fathers.

After Conversion

Galatians 2:20

I am crucified with Christ: nevertheless I live; yet not I, but Christ liveth in me: and the life which I now live in the flesh I live by the faith of the Son of God, who loved me, and gave himself for me.

After Jesus' baptism and Spirit infilling, His worldview changed from that of a lowly carpenter into a full blown Kingdom one. The Bible doesn't really give a lot of detail of His life before His baptism other than His birth, Him being a child prodigy and that He was a carpenter. Jesus didn't do anything miraculous in His life until He received the Holy Spirit. When Jesus received the Holy Spirit, His life drastically went to a totally different level.

After Jesus was baptised, He fasted for forty days and nights. He was then tempted by the devil and the first words He said were the Words of God.

Duet 8:3 - Matthew 4:4

Deut 6:16 - Matthew 4:7

Deut 6:13 - Matthew 4:10

Jesus' Language turned into the Fathers language because Jesus was consumed by the Spirit of God. He only spoke what God spoke and He only did what God did because He was consumed with the Language of the Spirit which is Life, Righteousness, Love; basically, the fruit of the Spirit.

All of the Bible characters spoke the Language of the Spirit, so their worldview was prophetic and powerful. Throughout the Bible, we are told to adopt the language of the Spirit and a spiritual worldview.

- Ezekiel - Priest - Saw God, Heaven and Angels - The past and the future

- Daniel - disciplined, God fearing young man saw angels, God, Jesus and the future

- Jerimiah - Priest - saw the future in great detail and heard the voice of God with pure clarity.

- David - prophet, king - saw the future and the Spirit realm

- Samuel - Priest - Saw in the Spirit and saw God with Clarity

There are many more Old Testament characters I could use as examples, like Moses, Enoch, Zechariah, Isaiah, etc.. but you can study them in your own time.

I just want you to get a full grasp of linguistic relativity and for you to understand that you become what you immerse yourself in. All of the prophets were infected by linguistic relativity, they could see God and the things of the Spirit clearer than anyone else.

The prophet Samuel had the ability to see people miles away, like Saul's father's lost donkeys.

1 Samuel 9:20

And as for thine asses that were lost three days ago, set not thy mind on them; for they are found. And on whom is all the desire of Israel? Is it not on thee, and on all thy father's house?

Elisha could also do this, he could see and hear things that others could not.

2 Kings 6:12

And one of his servants said, None, my lord, O king: but Elisha, the prophet that is in Israel, telleth the king of Israel the words that thou speakest in thy bedchamber.

In 2 Kings 6, it also speaks about the event with the Assyrians, the chariots of fire and Elisha's servant.

2 Kings 6:16-17

And he answered, Fear not: for they that be with us are more than they that be with them.

And Elisha prayed, and said, LORD, I pray thee, open his eyes, that he may see. And the LORD opened the eyes of the young man; and he saw: and, behold, the mountain was full of horses and chariots of fire round about Elisha.

But Jesus took this to a whole next level! Let's explore the depth of Jesus' spiritual and prophetic insight, because He was consumed with the Kingdom mindset.

Nathaniel By The Tree

John 1:48

Nathanael saith unto him, Whence knowest thou me? Jesus answered and said unto him, Before that Philip called thee, when thou wast under the fig tree, I saw thee.

The Woman By The Well

John 4:17-19

The woman answered and said, I have no husband. Jesus said unto her, Thou hast well said, I have no husband:

For thou hast had five husbands; and he whom thou now hast is not thy husband: in that saidst thou truly.

The woman saith unto him, Sir, I perceive that thou art a prophet.

The Donkey That Was Tied Up For His Triumphant Entry Into Jerusalem

Matthew 21:2

Saying unto them, Go into the village over against you, and straightway ye shall find an ass tied, and a colt with her: loose them, and bring them unto me.

The Man With Pitcher Of Water

Mark 14:13

And he sendeth forth two of his disciples, and saith unto them, Go ye into the city, and there shall meet you a man bearing a pitcher of water: follow him.

Jesus Knew That Judas Would Betray Him, 3 Years Before The Event

John 6:70

Jesus answered them, Have not I chosen you twelve, and one of you is a devil?

Just to name a few.

When you start to have the Kingdom Worldview, things begin to change in your life. If you want to dream about the prophetic or move in power, you have to understand "linguistic relativity", which means your life and mind will change according to what you say and what you immerse yourself in. To get a Kingdom Worldview, you have to do what Jesus, the Apostles and the Prophets of old did, which was to become obsessed with the things of God. You have to immerse yourself with Kingdom things and then you will begin to live life on a higher level.

BUT!!

Language relativity also works in the opposite way. If you immerse yourself with evil, then your worldview and the way you think will also be evil. This is exactly what is happening to many believers today; they have immersed themselves or have placed worldly things above the things of the Spirit, and likewise, they are suffering the consequences.

I know of people who always speak of "their sickness" and "their lack" and guess what? They are always sick and always experiencing lack! Their language is creating an unfavourable world for them to live in.

So, let's start walking in our New Kingdom Identity by changing the way we speak and act. Let us allow the culture of the Kingdom to transform us by surrendering our lives to our King.

----The End----

Or Not

YOUR TRUE KINGDOM IDENTITY

YOUR TRUE KINGDOM

Identity
THE MAJESTY WITHIN

BONUS

BONUS CHAPTER

The Identity Of Christ Is Your Identity

By Cassie J

This chapter is compiled from conversations I have had with Holy Spirit on His identity in me.

I will start this out with one such conversation:

"Whosoever I set free, is free indeed."

Wow, Holy Spirit! So, that means, whosoever I set free, is also free indeed?

"Yes, Cass. Remember, the Authority you have in me, is My Authority in you! So, when I tell you to set someone free from bondage, you can only do it by the authority I have placed in you."

John 5:26-27

For as the Father hath life in himself; so hath he given to the Son to have life in himself;

And hath given him authority to execute judgment also, because he is the Son of man.

2 Corinthians 10:8

For though I should boast somewhat more of our authority, which the Lord hath given us for edification, and not for your destruction, I should not be ashamed:

Holy Spirit has a way of starting conversations with me, anywhere, anytime, and this one started early one morning in February, 2023. I didn't get a chance to open my eyes or say good morning to Him, He just said His piece, as though I overslept. The relationship that we have is like that of a phone call which is left open-ended, in other words, you never hang up, so anyone can start talking about anything, at any time.

I am aware that the Bible, in the King James version, says 'make' and not 'set', however, Holy Spirit specifically said 'set' to me.

The point He was making was about His position in me, and what I do in that position.

To 'set' is to reposition something or someone that already exists, whilst to 'make' is to form or create something new that wasn't in existence; that is God's job, not ours. We can reposition (set) people free from accepting the lies of the devil, get them to change their thinking and focus by and with the help of Holy Spirit, but it is not our job to give them a new identity; that is God's job. He creates (makes) them that new identity in which they should live freely. We can only point them to that identity and reposition them to own it.

Seated Above In Power

Ephesians 1:19-21

And what is the exceeding greatness of his power to us-ward who believe, according to the working of his mighty power,

Which he wrought in Christ, when he raised him from the dead, and set him at his own right hand in the heavenly places,

Far above all principality, and power, and might, and dominion, and every name that is named, not only in this world, but also in that which is to come:

Ephesians 2:6

And hath raised us up together, and made us sit together in heavenly places in Christ Jesus:

"You are seated ABOVE in POWER," were the words I woke up to one morning. I pondered on them for a bit, then the revelation flowed.

Because we are born again, we sit at the Right hand (power) of the Father in our minds, in our beliefs, in our speaking and in our actions/reactions or our living. In other words, it is our lifestyle to live SEATED in Power.

We must NOT sit below the devil's position. He wants us to be ignorant of the truth of our positional authority and power over him, so that we will live and operate from a place which fears him. We are seated far above him; we are seated in heavenly places in Christ at the right hand of God!

As I have mentioned earlier, the right hand is God's Power, and we command from that position of power, taking control of our thoughts, our beliefs and our living. We take control of what we see (or focus on), what we hear (or tune into), what we speak and ultimately, what we have (or receive).

Matthew 21:21

Jesus answered and said unto them, Verily I say unto you, If ye have faith, and doubt not, ye shall not only do this which is done to the fig tree, but also if ye shall say unto this mountain, Be thou removed, and be thou cast into the sea; it shall be done.

Mark 11:23

For verily I say unto you, That whosoever shall say unto this mountain, Be thou removed, and be thou cast into the sea; and shall not doubt in his heart, but shall believe that those things which he saith shall come to pass; he shall have whatsoever he saith.

Wrong Identity Gives The Devil Bullying Rights

Walking in the wrong identity will allow the devil to bully us. For example, when we don't take captive every thought like we are instructed to in 2 Corinthians 10:5, we will be coerced into thinking about unfruitful things, like what others may or may not think about us. This then causes or forces us to act or react in a way, either to prove them wrong or in an attempt to cover the 'embarrassment'. The enemy then uses what you do, think or say against you to hold you in condemnation or shame/embarrassment.

2 Corinthians 10:5

Casting down imaginations, and every high thing that exalteth itself against the knowledge of God, and bringing into captivity every thought to the obedience of Christ;

Let me help you out a little; embarrassment is shame, and it is NOT our identity. It is a mindset which the enemy uses to get us to act, react, walk or talk outside of the mind of Christ. It is fleshly, and shame was nailed to the Cross, therefore, we should not operate in it. To live in or from embarrassment/shame, is to reject the sufferings of Christ as payment for our new identity, and in so doing, we would also reject this new identity. Our new, purchased identity is in the Mind of Christ.

1 Corinthians 2:16

For who hath known the mind of the Lord, that he may instruct him? but we have the mind of Christ.

Don't allow the enemy to cause you to walk in a weakened form of You, or the wrong identity, which he will use against you. Wake up to the Greatness of God inside of you! Don't you know that what you submerge yourself in is what you become? Don't lose your Kingdom identity to 'fit in'. Be strong in the Lord and in the power of His might. You have been empowered by Holy Spirit to be INFECTIOUS, not to be INFECTED! There is a Greater You, but you MUST believe it and stand in that Greaterness identity.

1 John 4:4

Ye are of God, little children, and have overcome them: because greater is he that is in you, than he that is in the world.

Here is a conversation I had with Holy Spirit on August 8th, 2023.

To give a bit of context, the morning of the 7th, when I asked Holy Spirit how He was, He replied, "Good Morning Daughter. I am Quick and Powerful". The thing is, what He says about Himself, I have to not only say it about myself, but I have to believe it!

Okay, now you know, this is how the conversation on the 8th went.

Holy Spirit, I liked what you said yesterday.

"I have an even better one today. Greatness belongs to God, Only God, and He gives it to whomsoever He chooses."

Now, you ponder on the above statement.

You were chosen by God and He has given YOU His Greatness!

Who Do You Say I Am?

The final conversation I will share here, is one where Holy Spirit spoke and I listened.

"Who do you say I am?" He asked me. Before I could think, He continued.

"Who you say I am, that is who You are! Therefore, if you are saying the wrong things about me, you are also saying the wrong things about yourself! To say the Truth about me, you have to search me and my Word, and you will find that both are one and the same; that is, the Spirit and the Word of God are one. They are the TRUTH, and when you find the Truth about me, you will know the Truth about yourself.

However, you can't know Truth unless you seek for Truth, and you will find Truth when He reveals Himself."

John 16:13

Howbeit when he, the Spirit of truth, is come, he will guide you into all truth: for he shall not speak of himself; but whatsoever he shall hear, that shall he speak: and he will shew you things to come.

Jeremiah 29:13

And ye shall seek me, and find me, when ye shall search for me with all your heart.

John 14:21

He that hath my commandments, and keepeth them, he it is that loveth me: and he that loveth me shall be loved of my Father, and I will love him, and will manifest myself to him.

Be Fruitful, Multiply And Replenish The Earth

Gen 1:28(a)

And God blessed them, and God said unto them, Be fruitful, and multiply, and replenish the earth, and subdue it:

What does this look like today? Well, in the Scripture which follows this, verse 29, God said He has given us every herb bearing seed, every tree which has fruit yielding seeds for our meat.

How powerful is that? Pertaining to our spiritual development, Everything we need to prosper, has been given to us by God through Christ Jesus, by the leading or working of Holy Spirit.

2 Peter 1:3-4

According as his divine power hath given unto us all things that pertain unto life and godliness, through the knowledge of him that hath called us to glory and virtue:

Whereby are given unto us exceeding great and precious promises: that by these ye might be partakers of the divine nature, having escaped the corruption that is in the world through lust.

We have been given Holy Spirit to lead or walk us through and to the person whom God called us to be - The Christ Character. His love, His grace, His patience, kindness, His thoughts, how He lives, and wants to live in and through us, and every other characteristic of Christ, forms our identity! Walking this way, leads us to become fruitful, leads us to multiply, leads us to replenish the Earth and to subdue it.

The same Grace and Forgiveness we received from God by His Spirit, because of the Blood of Christ, is the same Grace and Forgiveness we are to reciprocate to others.

The same Love which Christ loves us with, is the same Love that we Must/Should/Will love others with in order to fulfil that command.

This, also, can be clearly seen in:

John 13:34-35
A new commandment I give unto you, That ye love one another; as I have loved you, that ye also love one another.

By this shall all men know that ye are my disciples, if ye have love one to another.

Notice, He did not say to love one another how you want or when you feel like it! To break it down for you; He said the SAME way, with the SAME Love He loves you with, that is what you use to love others, EXACTLY how He loves you! In other words, you allow Him to love through you, with His Love, the way He loves.

Put your old character aside - forget the past ways of doing things, reach forward to the HIGHER New Character and identify with Christ's characteristics.

2 Corinthians 5:17
Therefore if any man be in Christ, he is a new creature: old things are passed away; behold, all things are become new.

1 John 3:1-3

Behold, what manner of love the Father hath bestowed upon us, that we should be called the sons of God: therefore the world knoweth us not, because it knew him not.

Beloved, now are we the sons of God, and it doth not yet appear what we shall be: but we know that, when he shall appear, we shall be like him; for we shall see him as he is.

And every man that hath this hope in him purifieth himself, even as he is pure.

These verses show us that we should be called God's sons (or daughters), and for us to be recognised as such, we have to learn and become who and what God says, with and by the guidance of Holy Spirit. He is the ONLY one who can and does lead us into ALL Truth, and He is the ONLY one who can train us to operate in the New Man, our new identity, from which we become Fruitful, Multiply and Replenish the Earth.

May your lives be transformed into your True Kingdom Identity.

YOUR TRUE KINGDOM IDENTITY

OTHER BOOKS BY
THE AUTHOR -
ROBERT JONES

ANOTHER BOOK BY ROBERT JONES

THE KINGDOM HANDBOOK

"Understand the Kingdom of Heaven and the Kingdom message."

There are so many different Bible teachings that have been taught from pulpits all around the world, since the inception of the Church. Some of these teachings are very good and some are very bad. In this book, we are going to cover the most important message ever presented to mankind and that is the teaching of the gospel of the Kingdom. This teaching of the gospel of the Kingdom was at the heart of Christ's ministry, but there is a major problem and that is, that most believers today, do not even know what the Kingdom of God is and how it operates. In this book, I will break down the Kingdom message into bite size pieces and when you understand and grasp the basics, your life will never be the same.

Available at amazon

ANOTHER BOOK BY ROBERT JONES

Spiritual WARFARE
What you don't know

It's time to press the master reset button on the topic of Spiritual Warfare. Over the decades, some of our leaders have twisted this teaching into something that's not even biblical. This book is all about addressing some of the errors and traditions that have been passed down over the years, which have gone unchecked and unscrutinised. There are so many things that we have been taught about spiritual warfare which neither Jesus nor the apostles did. The body of Christ needs a major paradigm shift so that we can wage a good warfare. It's time to relook at this subject with fresh eyes so that we can be more effective.

Available at amazon

Printed in Great Britain
by Amazon